WAYFARING

WAYFARING

A GOSPEL JOURNEY INTO LIFE

MARGARET SILF

with illustrations by **ROY LOVATT**

DARTON·LONGMAN+TODD

First published in 2001 by
Darton, Longman and Todd Ltd
1 Spencer Court
140-142 Wandsworth High Street
London SW18 4JJ

ISBN 0-232-52403-3

A catalogue record for this book is available from the British Library.

Designed and produced by Sandie Boccacci
using QuarkXPress on an Apple PowerMac 7500
Set in 11/14pt Bembo
Printed and bound in Great Britain by
The Cromwell Press, Trowbridge, Wiltshire

AD
MAJOREM
DEI
GLORIAM

CONTENTS

INTRODUCTION: WAYS NOT FOUND, BUT MADE

When I stand on the ridge of my favourite hillside in Wales, I can see many different 'ways' spread out below me – a major trunk road carving its way across the landscape, several substantial footpaths and cart tracks – and a whole network of thread-like trails traced across the flank of the hill, where sheep have picked a precarious way through the bracken.

Then Advent arrives and I hear, each year, the call to 'prepare the way of the Lord'. When I think of the trunk road across the Welsh countryside, this call seems like a massive undertaking that would need effort far beyond my own tiny resources to produce. But actually it might be something much more modest – more like the sheep trail through the bracken. A way that is quite clearly visible from the brow of the hill, but a way that was made simply by one creature walking one personal route through the undergrowth. Perhaps the way of the Lord might allow for trails like these, as well as for the heavy goods lanes along the juggernaut routes to God.

This book is an invitation to walk your own living pathway in the companionship of Jesus of Nazareth. Ways are made very simply. We don't have to accomplish some feat of heavy engineering. All we have to do is put one foot in front of the other, and *walk* them. To walk with Jesus through his lived ministry, through his suffering and death, and into his resurrected life and discover for ourselves what it really means for us, and asks of us. It is an invitation to become a *wayfarer*, who, simply by walking the way alongside the One who *is* the Way, and in loving relationship with fellow wayfarers, will also become a *waymaker* for others.

The path that lies ahead is one particular way of exploring the Christian gospel. It is an experiential journey through the events and stories that are our common Christian heritage and our map and compass for the route, whatever our tradition. However, those who are at all familiar with the spirituality of St Ignatius Loyola will immediately recognise his inspiration in the shape and nature of this particular journey, and in the way the meditations are focused. The 'Spiritual Exercises' of St Ignatius have become, for many, a powerful and effective guide to the making of this Gospel journey in faith and prayer. The pattern of this book follows the dynamic of these 'Exercises', as a framework for exploring what it means to participate, through our own lives, in the life, death and resurrection of the Lord.

Though its inspiration is Ignatian, its language is not. The only reference you will find to 'Ignatius' or his 'Exercises' is here in the Introduction. I make no apology for this, as I am sure that the spirit of Ignatius is much bigger than his label, just as I have no doubt that the Kingdom of God is infinitely greater than all the formulations of organised religion.

This is a pilgrimage journey, not a tourist outing. It is a journey that changes the traveller, a process that shapes the soul in ways we cannot predict. In my diary I have a slip of paper with the following text:

The future is not some place we are going to but one we are creating.
The paths to it are not found but made,
and the making of those pathways
changes both the maker and the destination.

I wish I knew who wrote these words, so that I could thank him or her for expressing so succinctly the kernel of this mysterious process of discovering and *real*-ising the deepest truth at the core of our being. This book is about the creating of the future, about the making of the ways which lead to where we long to be, the wayfaring that changes us, the wayfarers, and the 'waymaking' that shapes our destination even as we walk. It is about the co-creating of a Kingdom, whose 'king' walks with us.

In many ways this book is a companion volume to *Landmarks: An Ignatian Journey*, and it is intended to be used in the same way, taking each step gently, prayerfully, and personally, lingering with anything that speaks to your heart especially, and leaving aside anything that does not. For each reader this journey of prayer will be different, yet all our pathways are searching out the same destination in their own ways. If you have used *Landmarks*, then *Wayfaring* will accompany you further on your way. Linger, especially, over the exercises included (in boxed text) along the way, and try to enter into them in prayer, and in the context of your own story and circumstances, noticing your responses and reactions. Where scriptural reflection is suggested, try to go beyond merely 'reading' to a genuine personal participation in the various Gospel encounters.

The Gospel journey explored in *Wayfaring* does not assume any previous familiarity with *Landmarks* or with any other book. It welcomes equally those who are just beginning to explore the spiritual journey and those who are already seasoned travellers, those of all Christian traditions and those of none, those 'inside' and those 'outside' the 'church', those who have long cherished the wisdom of Ignatius and those who have never heard of him. My prayer is only that all our wayfaring remains faithful to the spirit of the One who calls himself the Way.

My special thanks are due to those who have guided me along these pathways, and who remain my loved and trusted companions of the journey. I would like, especially, to express my warmest gratitude to Brian McClorry SJ, Gerry Hughes SJ and Michael Ivens SJ. Thank you, Brian, for helping me to pick my way through the bracken of God's mountainside when I scarcely knew how to walk, for the gift of your continuing friendship, and for all your comments and advice in the shaping of this book. Thank you, Gerry, for walking the path of the *Exercises* with me, and for your loving companionship and tireless encouragement in the living and the praying that gave rise to this book. Thank you, Michael, for our 'Ignatian conversations' and your time and patience in reading and commenting on the drafts of this book, but also for your unquenchable enthusiasm and inspiration.

Thank you to Teresa Foster, for your gentle, loving and challenging companionship through so many years, to all at St Beuno's Ignatian Spirituality Centre in North Wales, especially those who have accompanied my retreats, to my own faith community at the Keele University chaplaincy, to Catherine Lack and Bill Thomas, our present chaplains, whose ministry never fails to inspire and to challenge me, to my friends and fellow pilgrims in the Manresa Link, to the late Donald Nicholl, whose presence is still very much alive in my life and in this book, and to my personal 'soul-friends' who have shared something of their journeys with me or allowed me to share something of mine with them.

And thank you to the hundreds of people I have had the joy and privilege of meeting in recent times, from every shade of opinion and practice along the spectrum of Christian tradition, and, indeed, from beyond the boundary fences of the 'Church'. You have been a source of immense energy and inspiration to my own journeying – springs of living water that refresh me at every stop along the way.

Not least, I would like to thank my husband, Klaus, for his generous support and invaluable help in facilitating retreats and workshops and for his tolerance of my travels and other 'writer's habits', and my daughter, Kirstin, for the countless ways in which she inspires and revitalises me.

And finally, my thanks go to my friends and colleagues at Darton, Longman and Todd, especially Katie Worrall, Helen Porter and Kathy Dyke, for all their work and encouragement in the long process of turning first thoughts into printed words, and to Roy Lovatt, for his inspired illustrations. Roy was my colleague for many years when we were writing technical manuals for a computer manufacturer. It is a particular joy to see that working relationship move on into the much more interesting terrain of the spiritual journey.

I would like to wish you a safe journey along these Gospel roads, but 'safety' is not always compatible with the ways of God or with the adventure of prayer. And so I wish you, instead, a graced, and a joyful journey through the darkness and the light, the rockfaces and the mountain-top wonderment. Thank you for allowing me to journey with you through these pages as we explore the landscape of God, and may God give us the grace to share the fruits of our journeying with each other and with God's world.

A Way that shapes both
the traveller and the terrain

1. SEEDS OF GOD

This morning I went into my daughter's bedroom. She is nineteen now and away at university. Her room at home is full of expressions of who she is. There are posters on the wall, books on the shelves, clothes in the cupboard, CDs in the rack and ornaments that she has chosen, or been given. Everything has something to say about her life, her friends, her unique presence in the world.

Beyond the few square yards of her room, the network of her life reaches, one might say, to the ends of the earth. To her family and friends in various parts of Europe, North America, Asia and Australia, and to her circle of companions whose own lives are just coming to blossom, like an exuberant springtime, to grow into their own kinds of fruitfulness.

Yet, twenty years ago, she was a single cell! She could have been examined under a microscope. She could have been placed on a pinhead, along with all her classmates. Such a short time ago she was a microscopic particle of creation, and now she is a fully developed human being on the threshold of her adult life, with the potential to do almost anything she chooses.

Everything in this room expresses relationships she has formed, and interests she has pursued. Her presence in the world has reached out in countless different ways to affect the lives of others, as their lives have affected her. Above all, she has injected a charge of her own unique power of love into the world. She has energised creation with her own enthusiasm for living. She has become an essential node in the web of life, so complex that none but God knows its detail and potential. She has inspired love. And love has inspired her.

As I stood in her room this morning I was overwhelmed by the miracle of life, that begins from almost nothing and has the potential to grow into almost everything. Each human life reflects the same pattern as the universe itself – beginning from a single point, infinitesimally small, and expanding outwards, constantly revealing more and more of its immeasurable potential.

In my purse I carry a photograph of my daughter. It reminds me of how she looked at the moment the photo was taken, and I value it. But it can never capture more than the tiniest fragment of who she really is. That has to be experienced, in real life and in genuine interaction, and even then we can only begin to touch the full reality of each other.

Perhaps what any of us knows of each other – even of our friends and closest acquaintances – is more like the photo than the reality. We experience each other in three dimensions. The reality, surely, reaches out into infinite dimensions, and is rooted deep into that first single point from which our being sprang. We hear each other's words, sighs and songs, but only on a narrow waveband that our ears can receive. The full reality of life's song is surely being broadcast on infinite wavelengths. What we think we see and hear is not only partial, but can even be very misleading. We make judgements about each other on very scant evidence, and we even pass judgement on ourselves, reducing ourselves to an image glimpsed in the distorting mirror of our own perceptions.

Before we set out on the journey mapped out by this book, we pause for a while to let God deepen that shallow picture we have of ourselves and of each other, and to open up just a little of the infinite treasure in the heart of our true selves, that only God is fully aware of.

Nathanael and the pink elephants

One of the Lord's first friends can give us a few clues about this process. Let's stop by with Nathanael, one lazy morning in the sun. Things are stirring around Galilee. A new teacher has been attracting interest and a small band of followers has been gathering. Nathanael is sitting under a fig tree (John 1:43-50). Maybe he was doing what a good young Jew should have been doing – meditating on the Scriptures. Or maybe he was up to no good at all, there under the fig tree. You can fill in the details as you wish. John leaves us free to speculate.

Whatever he is doing there, Jesus notices him, but Nathanael is unaware of this, and continues in his reverie until his friend Philip arrives on the scene, out of breath and bursting with excitement. 'Nathanael,' he interrupts unceremoniously. 'We've found the one the prophets spoke about, the promised one. He's Joseph's son, from Nazareth.'

Nathanael is visibly under-impressed by this news. 'Nazareth?' he retorts. 'You must be joking! When did anything good ever come out of Nazareth?' 'Come and see for yourself,' Philip replies. Nathanael rouses himself from his pitch under the fig tree and takes up Philip's invitation. Jesus sees them coming in the distance and his comment carries across the still air to reach them before they arrive. 'This is a true Israelite,' he says. 'There is nothing false in him.' Nathanael is justifiably taken aback. 'How did you know me?' he asks Jesus. 'I saw you under the fig tree,' comes the simple reply. Bowled over by Jesus' ability to see straight to the heart of things, Nathanael responds in kind: 'Teacher, you are the Son of God. You are the King of Israel!'

I had been reflecting on this scene from the Gospel one morning, and later in the day I happened to come across another story. I learned that there is a region somewhere in Africa that has pink elephants! The elephants are pink because there is something in the soil that gives the vegetation a pinkish pigmentation, and this in turn turns into pink elephant. They are what they eat. And if what they eat is pink, so are they!

I couldn't help connecting this useless piece of information with the story of Nathanael. He had decided in advance that 'nothing good could come out of Nazareth'. Have we never made that kind of judgement ourselves? Don't expect much of him, he's from a broken home, or she's from an immigrant family. He's disabled, he won't be able to help, or she's 'only a housewife' so don't expect intellectual leaps from her! Not to mention our own pet regional prejudices! Yet, like the elephants, we are formed and coloured by the circumstances in which we are planted. The contrast between Nathanael's attitude and Jesus' insight is a crucial one. Nathanael sees just one fact and builds up a whole wrong picture from it. Jesus sees just one 'snapshot' of a human person and sees the whole, true picture deep inside that person's being.

Read the story of Nathanael's meeting with Jesus, in John 1:43-50. Try to imagine that you are personally present to the scene. Where do you find yourself? How do you feel? Listen to the conversations, between Nathanael and Philip, and between Nathanael and Jesus. Is there anything you would like to say yourself? Suppose Jesus had noticed *you* there under the fig tree? What do you think he might have said about you?

Like the pink elephants, the visible 'you' is coloured by the circumstances in which you live. But God sees the true colours of your invisible being. Others see just the snapshot view of you. God sees the true reality, not only of who you are, but of the person you have the potential to become. How do you feel about these two different 'pictures' of yourself? Is there any area of your life where you feel you are being judged by an outer image that is not a true reflection of your real self? You might ask God, in your prayer, to open the eyes of your heart to see the deeper reality of those close to you, and also to glimpse, and to cherish, the deeper reality of your own true self, which is known fully only to God.

The way that lies ahead of us is a journey of the heart – the journey of our true selves towards the true centre and source of all Being. God has already recognised us in our true colours and in the fullness of our potential. He invites us to 'come and see' what he is about, just as Nathanael was invited. For our part, he asks us to say 'Yes' to the presence of God within us and to the growth of that particle of his presence – perhaps no bigger than the single cell from which we sprang – into everything that God alone knows it is capable of becoming. We can only say that 'Yes' when we have glimpsed the infinite value and beauty of the treasure of Godself within us.

In practice, this 'Yes' often turns out to be far harder to say than we could have imagined. We begin by looking at some of the reasons behind our reluctance to acknowledge the Godseed in our hearts.

Paying life's rental

Why am I always so busy? What am I actually always so busy doing? What happens to the passing days, so that when I write to a friend I always seem to start off by apologising for the fact that I haven't written for I don't know how many weeks?

I've often asked myself questions like these and I've often heard others ask them too. But I haven't very often sat still for long enough to begin to hear any kind of answer. The other day it was different. A friend was telling me how busy he had been, and how little time there had been for any kind of prayer or reflection since we had last met. The busy-ness, he realised, came about largely because he found it very difficult to say 'No' to whatever anyone might ask of him. I found myself listening to what could just as well have been my own inner self speaking. Then I surprised myself by responding with some more questions: 'Why do we do it? Why do we fill up our every minute with busy-ness? Why do we keep on and on saying "Yes", when sometimes it might be wiser to say a loving "No"?'

A longish silence ensued. We sat pondering the real roots of our frenetic activity, and we came to some rather shocking conclusions.

- We discovered something inside us that suggested we were only worth-while, as human beings, if we were constantly pleasing people.
- We found that we felt guilty if, at the end of the day, we had nothing to show for our twenty-four hours' lease of life.
- We realised that we felt that we were only entitled to occupy our little plot of earth on the condition that we earned our rental.

Then my friend put his finger right onto the pulse of the matter. 'I guess,' he said, 'that I can't imagine that there is anything of intrinsic value within me just as I am. I only feel I have any value when I can count my takings in the currency of "jobs well done", "people more or less well pleased" and "affirmation earned".'

The 'No' beneath all the 'Yesses'

This was actually a quite terrifying admission, yet, as I well knew, it was one that many, if not all of us, would have to acknowledge as a characteristic of the shaky foundations upon which we build our lives. Underneath all those eager (or sometimes resentful) 'Yesses', there lurks a deeper 'No'.

This uneasy relationship between my tendency to say 'Yes' to everyone and everything, until I become totally overloaded, and the deep-down 'No', was brought home to me quite dramatically one afternoon. I was visiting a friend who was dying. As I sat down at his bedside he completely took the wind out of my sails by telling me how sorry he was to hear that I had not managed to take the few days' break I had been planning the previous week. It didn't feel like an important issue to me, and I dismissed it. I hadn't been able to go because such-and-such had cropped up, and I had needed to do this, that and the other. He listened patiently while I offered my 'excuses' for not having had a holiday. Then he looked straight into my eyes and said: 'Margaret, sometimes too many "Yesses" are concealing a deeper "No"!' For just a fleeting moment, I had the feeling that not just my friend, but God himself was looking into my soul. We both recognised something of the hidden nature of the deep-down 'No'. He took my hands in his. I knew that he was reading me like a book, yet still completely loving all he saw. The words were simple: 'I *know*, my love, I *know*,' he murmured.

The two possibilities, of *knowing* and *loving*, side by side, sliced open my defences and my eyes filled with tears. I realised then that it was an even more awesome thing to be unconditionally loved, than to be totally known.

I think that it was on that afternoon that I began to glimpse the real nature of the 'No'. It was about that deep-rooted conviction that nothing in me has intrinsic value, and I am only worth what I can do, and, more-over, what I am seen to be doing! 'Conviction' is the right word. I was beginning to see that I had convicted myself of worthlessness. No one else had convicted me, least of all God. On the contrary, all the people I was so busy trying to please were equally busy justifying their own existence and implicitly convicting themselves of worthlessness.

I remembered the look in the eyes of my dying friend, the look of knowledge enfolded in love. I remembered how often I had heard the affirmation of God's love, in Scripture, in liturgy, and from wise counsel-lors. Why did such affirmation lodge solidly in my head and refuse to move to my heart? Why was this stubborn atheist deep in the heart of me so determined to reject the possibility that at the core of my being I might be an object of God's unconditional love, with no requirement to prove myself!

Read and reflect on God's promise expressed in Isaiah 43:1-7. Listen to these words, spoken directly and personally to you by the God who created you and sustains you in being. How do you wish to respond?

From Being to Doing

The more I pondered this conversation about the reasons for our in-ordinate busy-ness, and the underlying feelings that we need to please people in order to have any value, the more I began to wonder whether this was an almost universal phenomenon. For example, I personally know almost no one who, when congratulated on using some particular gift effectively, will not shyly deny or modestly minimise it, or pass the credit on to someone else.

It almost seems as though we don't know how to deal with the possibility that we are unconditionally loved, just as we are, and that our many efforts to please others and even to 'do God's work' make not a scrap of difference to his love for us. So we dismiss the possibility. And when we do so, we dismiss something of the potential of God to become God in our own lives. We stifle the growth of the unique Godseed of which we are the chosen carrier. We refuse to trust that our Being is more real than all our Doing. We put the cart firmly before the horse, forgetting that 'being' always comes before 'doing' and that 'doing' is a consequence, not a cause, of 'being'.

There are times, however, when Being takes precedence over Doing. One such time seems to be in the early years of childhood. Unless my memory fails me, in the early years of a child's life, he will tell you 'what he wants to *be*, when he grows up.' But the time comes, probably in the early years of secondary schooling, when the question changes to 'What are you going to *do* when you grow up?' What we are going to do gets mixed in with what exams we are going to take, what courses we are going to pursue, what qualifications we are going to work for. From then on, we will almost invariably introduce ourselves and each other in terms of our job, especially if that job carries a salary and some status.

Another of the times when Being reasserts itself over 'doing' is when we lose our ability to 'do' and are forced, by circumstances, back into the mode of simply 'being'. This can happen through illness, redundancy, or the failure of our support systems in some way, locking us into immobility, or perhaps more acceptably, during a period of seclusion such as we might voluntarily enter in a retreat.

But perhaps the best approximation to the perfection of just 'being' is reached when we are in love. Time ceases to drive us and for a few sweet hours, or perhaps months, if we are lucky, we desire nothing more than to be with the beloved. We have nothing to prove, because we know ourselves to be loved by this one other human being. That is all. That is enough. It feels like the fullness of life itself. It is possibly the nearest human analogy we can find for the deep desire we cherish in our hearts, to be held in love, just as we are, by the Lord of all creation.

Jesus tells us that in order to enter the Kingdom we must become as little children. Perhaps one aspect of this call is to recover the sense of Being, which is our birthright, and to let go of the compulsion for Doing, which has taken us over more and more, choking to death that first awareness of being loved just for our own sake, and being able to love others just because they are who they are.

Can you remember being asked, as a child, 'What do you want to **be** when you grow up?' What did you reply at that age?

When do you think that the question changed into 'What do you want to **do**?' When did you slip from Being to Doing? And how did Doing manage to take over so completely?

Try writing down a few of the things you wanted to 'be' when you were a child. Now write a separate list of the things you wanted to 'do', once you realised that you were going to have to work for a living. How do the two lists relate to each other?

Can you see any ways in which your childhood dreams have been turned into reality in ways that perhaps surprise you?

But true Being expresses itself in the best kind of 'Doing' and 'Making'. It's interesting – and revealing – to notice that we often feel most happy with our 'being', when we are doing well those things that we feel we are really called to do. You might like to reflect on this fact, and just take a few moments to notice those things in your own life that make you feel more truly who you are, when you are doing, or making, them well.

A process of 'becoming' or a feat of engineering?

So we are caught up in our 'busy-ness'. And we are more than a little wary, perhaps, of the possibility of being loved unconditionally, just as we are. In fact, the whole challenge of 'being' is much harder to handle than the many ways in which we can channel our compulsion to be 'doing'.

We are about to embark on a journey with Jesus, through the years of his lived ministry, through the days of his Passion, through the hours of his death, into the infinity of his resurrection. This journey will challenge us over and over again to 'be' with him, and it will pay little heed to all that we think we are 'doing' for him. Quite the reverse: it will gradually uncover, if we let it, just what *he* is doing in *us*. To allow him to do that 'doing', we will have to learn how to 'be' again, just as he told us.

This first stage of the journey calls us to recover the value of our Being. Many things may be militating against this perception of ourselves. Certainly we live in a society that measures us by our achievements. More subtly, and more dangerously, our religious structures tend to underscore the same message. The 'achievement' in this case is a passport to 'heaven', which we are misled to believe, in varying degrees by different traditions, that we can gain by a series of good works and holy obligations. While it is true that no Church would suggest that we are 'saved' by anything but the grace of God, there is nevertheless often a discrepancy between the *words* of 'the Church' and its *body language*. We are *told* that we are all loved sinners. Yet the structure of our religious institutions sets before us a pyramid model reflecting a 'building', man-made in every sense, with its own inbuilt power systems and 'hierarchies of holiness'. This journey through the Gospel story assumes a different model – an organic one, which Jesus himself revealed to us. It is the model of the Kingdom as the Body of Christ, in which every creature is called to be a living cell.

Bodies grow and evolve. Modern biology tells us that creation is a self-renewing organism, constantly seeking to generate new life. We are living beings on a living planet in a living, changing, dynamic universe. Buildings are static. They don't tolerate mistakes. Once a mistake is built into the house, you have to live with it, or knock the house down and start again. Bodies are relational: they live and grow by relating to each other, continually giving rise to new forms of life. Buildings tend to be self-sufficient. And when their time is over, they disintegrate, leaving only empty space.

Dynamic or static? Inter-related, or self-sufficient? Inclusive or exclusive? Being or Doing? Which model speaks more profoundly to your heart and your experience?

God described himself, to Moses, as 'I AM WHO I AM' (Exodus 3:13-15). *I AM* is about being alive – not about earning our existence. Take some time to reflect on what makes you feel alive. This will help you to see more clearly what kind of reflection of God is growing from your personal Godseed. Try looking back over the past twenty-four hours. Don't make any judgements on what you find, simply notice it. In all the experience of the past day, what stands out as something that made you feel 'more alive'? What seemed to give you energy? Draw up a list of the life-giving things you find. Now notice the things that seemed to drain you of life and energy. Repeat the exercise regularly, and see whether any patterns emerge. How might you nurture the life-giving things? How might you use the energy they generate in you to do those necessary things that fail to give you life?

A cell in the Body of Christ

Jesus revealed much of the meaning of the Father by telling stories. He told people the God Story, but he told it in images and narratives that they would readily recognise from their own stories. Indeed, I have heard 'church' defined as 'a space where we tell our stories and break bread'.

When I reflect on Jesus as the one who invites us to tell our stories in the light of his story, and to break bread with him, to be his *companions*, I begin to see Jesus himself as the First Cell of God's Kingdom on earth. We could perhaps envisage Jesus as God's Seed falling into our earth, in order to bring the Kingdom to birth.

Cells grow by division. Jesus 'divided' himself by sharing his love and his meaning with a small group of friends. He shared himself by telling them new aspects of his story day by day, and by illustrating his truth in actions of healing, forgiving, consoling, challenging, teaching and praying. He broke his story up for them, as the roots of an iris might be broken up in order to spread and multiply. He planted the Godseed in their hearts, so that it might grow into the Kingdom.

And when the time was come, he allowed himself to be literally broken on the cross. He compared his sacrifice to the breaking of bread, so that all who understood his meaning would take into their own being the fragments of God himself and allow these fragments to become living loaves for others.

We could even call this first group of friends a 'starter kit' for the Kingdom, as a lump of leavened dough starts the next loaf going. Now, two thousand years later, the circle of the Kingdom has moved outwards unimaginably, and we are on its boundaries – called to continue that sharing and growing and spreading, each in our own way.

What might it mean, to be a 'cell in the Body of Christ'? A cell is an amazing entity. It has at least these characteristics:

- It contains the encoded reality of the whole organism of which it is a part.
- It contains the programme of its own specific role within that living organism.
- It communicates continually with the other cells in the body.
- It knows when to die.

If we apply this to our own bodies, we know, for example, that a cell from any part of us contains the DNA of the whole of us. Thus, a DNA sample from any part of us, enables us to be uniquely identified. We know, too, that a cell from, say, our ear, 'knows' that it has to become a bit more ear, and not a fingernail. It knows the programme for its own 'becoming'. And by means of countless electrical pulses every second, it remains in perfect and balanced communication with all other cells. Finally, it knows that it is part of a long continuum of being. A cell that does not die when its lifespan is complete becomes cancerous.

If we now apply this understanding to ourselves as 'cells in the Body of Christ', we begin to realise that our lives carry within them, *at the core of our being*:

- the encoded reality that identifies us with the fullness of all creation and its creator;
- the personal 'programme' of our own role within that Body;
- the means of remaining in creative communion with each other;
- the recognition that our personal being is part of a process that asks us to receive life from all that has gone before, and to allow life to pass on beyond ourselves.

Part of the purpose of the journey we are making through this book is to seek to discover our personal programme. In accompanying Jesus through the Gospel story, we ask for the grace to recognise and respond to the unique and personal role of our own life within the Kingdom, and also to see how our own life reflects something of the mystery and the meaning of the whole Body. It is a journey shaped by the underlying longing that when our earthly lives are over, the Kingdom may be a little closer to its coming than when we were born.

But first God calls us into a deeper awareness of the wonder and the beauty concealed at the heart of our being and the being of all creation – a beauty that even the ravages of sin have not been able to obliterate.

Jesus said: 'Anyone who has seen me has seen the Father. I am in the Father and the Father is in me.' And later 'On that day you will know that I am in my Father and you in me and I in you' (John 14:9, 10, 20). Jesus, the 'first cell' of the Body of Christ, contains the encoded reality of God himself. He goes on to tell us that if our lives are incorporated into his, then we too will hold the reality of God within us.

Suppose he were to say to you: 'Anyone who has seen and really recognised *you*, will have glimpsed something of the reality of God.' How would you feel? How would you react? What, if anything, would you want to say to him?

Your personal 'cell'

The journey that lies ahead of us in this book is a kind of spiritual marathon. It will invite us to be participants, in our prayer and in our living, in the events of Jesus' earthly ministry, his suffering, death and resurrection. Preparing to run a physical marathon entails long months of training. A runner's stamina will be challenged by the demands of the course. It would be foolish to set out seriously to complete the distance without the basic level of fitness for the task ahead.

Our Gospel journey is likewise going to make demands on us. Demands of truth and integrity, and of courage to face our own darkness. It too requires a basic level of 'fitness', but this kind of fitness isn't something that we can train ourselves into or do anything to achieve, and in ourselves we would never be fit enough even to begin. It is simply the acceptance that there is a fragment of God embedded in our hearts. We might call it our personal 'cell', the core of our being, or our deepest self. All that is asked of us is that we trust that God himself is becoming incarnate in our personal life story and that he is continually loving us into life, whether we think we deserve it or not. It is the simplest thing to ask. To embrace the truth of it is perhaps the hardest thing we will ever do.

The reflections in the remainder of this chapter are invitations to take hold, in whatever way feels right for you, of the stupendous fact that God *knows* you totally, and *loves* you unconditionally. When that certainty starts to take root in your being, then all the challenges that follow are the stages of the unstoppable growth of Godself in your life.

A pebble on the beach

I have a pebble that I treasure. It is an agate stone, but from the outside it is very much 'just another pebble on the beach'. Just another rock to stub your toe on.

Yet this little stone thrills me, which is why I bought it, very cheaply, from a Mediterranean market stall. It thrills me because, when I turn it over, I am face to face with the most amazing beauty. It has been sliced

Just another pebble on the beach... and also a unique manifestation of God

open and polished, exposing a world inside itself that takes my breath away, and revealing layer upon layer of its own 'becoming'.

For me, this pebble is an icon of each one of us. An image of the layers of our being and the patterns of our growth, a pointer to vast unfathomed depths of ourselves that we cannot see, or even guess at, and a reminder of our intimate relationship with everything that is.

But the secret of my inner 'pebble' is only revealed when it is sliced open. For this to happen, someone, outside and beyond myself, must know me with a knowledge deeper than any I could have myself – deep enough to recognise the reality beneath this hard, unassuming shell that disguises, yet contains, me. And for my part, I must let the breaking open happen, and I must *trust* that it will be a breaking into birth, not death.

My outer shell, like the pebble's outer surface, is tough and weather-worn – the most recent accretion upon a long process of mystery. Maybe the latest layer of anything, whether of a pebble or of a nation, *has* to be tough to protect the deeper mystery. But it also, ultimately, has to be humble enough to be broken open, just as my pebble had to be sliced open to reveal its innermost story.

Just one single slice of this agate stone reads like the story of the whole earth. It makes me realise that a geologist is as much a poet and a mystic as any of the people who sit on my bookshelves at home. Stunning beauty, totally unexpected. No one could ever guess that such a stone could contain something so sublime. In my imagination I can almost hear the gasp of amazement from the first person to slice into an agate stone and find what I see now. In that gasp of breath-held wonder I feel deeply connected to that first geologist. We are just two of the countless multitude of God's discoverers, two lives through whom the divine breath has passed, and linked for eternity, by this little stone.

The second thing I see is the layering. Layer upon layer reflecting the same patterns, but in subtly changing shades and colours. The pattern revealed is made up of *fractals* – the same patterns that physicists and mathematicians are discovering in the equations that describe the way the universe evolves and holds together. Here, in a pebble, I can gaze at mathematical equations and at the layered seams of all our Becoming, and touch the mystery of this eternal one-ness of all our attempts to understand God's creation.

The pebble has been sliced in just one way, out of a multitude of possibilities. Any other angle would have revealed a different pattern, yet one formed in harmony with these same fundamental shapes, reflecting both the unique nature of this particular pebble and the universal laws of all creation. My life, too, my little container of being, could have been sliced in any of an infinite number of ways. My circumstances could have worked out so differently. Just one different choice at any one point along the way could have resulted in a very different pattern when my 'stone' was sliced. Yet whatever pattern had emerged, it would have revealed, in its own unique way, the truth about me and a fragment of the truth about all that is.

It makes me realise that the particular ways in which my set of circumstances are working out are perhaps no more important, in themselves, than the way in which a pack of cards falls when shuffled. Some hands will be short-term winners, others will be short-term losers – but all will be long-term revealers, and birth-givers.

And then we come to the deep centre of the stone. When I look at my pebble, I see, at the heart of its innermost void, a cluster of precious crystals. It feels like gazing up into a star-filled sky and knowing a moment of unity with the dark universe – or, gazing in the opposite direction, into the depths of my own being. Innermost and outermost. All One in God. Alone in the empty space in the heart of my own insignificant pebble. All-One at the centre beyond all the fractal patterns and all the still unrealised permutations of circumstance.

We are held and cherished, like pebbles on the beach of being, while the tides wash over us. We are held and cherished when the blades of pain and fear slice through us. Birth pains. For reasons that are still enclosed in mystery, this seems to be the only way in which the beauty and the truth inside us can be revealed. And we are called to hold and cherish every other pebble on the beach, because in the core of our being every single one of us contains the mystery of itself, and the mystery of all that IS.

Imagine your Being as an agate stone. What layers do you see in it? What is the outer crust like? What layers of experience have formed you into who you are today? How do you imagine the crystals at the heart of your being? What 'slicing' happened in your life to open up the beauty of your stone? How has that beautiful, exposed inner self been polished since then? How do you feel about it?

If you feel drawn to do so, try creating a picture of your inner agate stone, with its different layers and colours and its innermost jewel.

Share your feelings about your 'pebble' with a friend, and listen with your heart as your friend describes his/her own agate stone.

A pearl in the oyster

When I was pregnant I entertained myself one morning by browsing through the books of babies' names at a local bookstore. In the course of my searching I read through the meanings and origins of my own name, which derives from the Greek word meaning 'pearl'. It was there that I came across this delightful legend of how the pearl came to be.

The story told how the oyster had been lodged in the sandy sea-bed,

moving aimlessly in the mud at the depths of the ocean. But one night
there was a full moon, and the brilliant light penetrated even those dark
depths. The oyster was profoundly attracted by the mysterious glow, and
drawn, as by a magnet, to the surface of the water and the source of the
light. As she broke the surface, she was overcome by the glory of the light,
now sensed with a directness that had been impossible under water. It was
a glory and a power that invited her, irresistibly, to open herself to its overwhelming presence. Her shell loosened under its spell, just enough to trap
a fragment of the moonlight within her innermost self for all eternity.

She was a mortal creature, and her vision could only last for a fleeting,
eternal moment. The waves drew her down again to the sea-bed. But the
pearl was formed within her, conceived in the heavenly encounter, and it
would grow, slowly, imperceptibly, through all her years, until one day, the
One who knew what she contained, would take her between his fingers,
open the shell, and gaze with love upon the pearl that he had made.

The God-Within, loved into being
by the God-Beyond

This legend of the pearl is another way that helps me to take hold of the truth that in each of us there is a fragment of the Being whom we call God. When we reflect on the stirrings we feel within our own depths, we know that we, too, have been touched by the brilliance of a presence beyond our understanding. There have been moments when we knew, with heart-knowledge, that we were a part of something, or Someone, infinitely greater than ourselves. In responding to that presence, however inadequately, the hard crusts of our being have been opened, ever so slightly, to let in something of the presence of God. Once that has happened, the Godseed within us begins to grow into the unique fragment of Godself that our lives are destined to reveal.

And just as the agate stone had to be sliced open, and painfully polished, to reveal its inner beauty, and the oyster shell has to be prised open to reveal the pearl, so life will sooner or later slice through our comforts and securities to reveal the mystery of the core of our being.

The legend of the pearl reveals a spiritual truth. Science gives us another 'take' on the mystery of the pearl. From science we learn that pearls are formed as a reaction by the oyster to the presence of an irritant grain of sand in its tender inner parts, a grain of sand which it tries to coat with a substance which gradually creates the pearl. So too, perhaps, the beauty within us is also the fruit of the irritant grain of sand that we would some-times do anything to be rid of. Our worst pain may be creating that deep beauty which is becoming a reflection of God's own Being.

In a quiet corner of the house I have an oyster shell, close to a candle and a cross, to remind me that my own inner pearl is known and loved by God, who conceived it in me by the power of his love, and to remind me that the circumstances that cause me the most pain and heartache may well be the grain of sand that is continuing to bring my pearl to birth.

Can you remember any experience in your life that could be described in terms like those used in the legend of the pearl? Have you any memory of being mysteriously 'opened to God' in ways that were not your own devising? Sometimes the simplest events or encounters have this kind of power: a moment of exquisite awareness of creation, for example, or a pure shaft of love. Relive, in your imagination, any such moment that you recall, and ask God to confirm and strengthen the growth that he began in you then.

Reflect on how your innermost being first caught the shaft of Godlight. You might like to notice and acknowledge your own life's irritant 'grains of sand', around which your pearl of great price is forming and growing.

A grain of dust

Sometimes we don't even feel like 'a pebble on the beach'. When we look up into a starry sky, for example, or reflect on the origins of the universe, as we understand them, we feel so insignificant as to be eminently forgettable. Can it be, then, that a passing speck of life on a minor planet on the edge of a remote galaxy in an uncharted universe, which may itself be one universe among many – can it be that such a speck of life as we are can ever be in relationship with all that is? The thought can be terrifying, but our intuition suggests that there may be wonder on the far side of terror.

The writer of the apocryphal Book of Wisdom speaks of the world in these terms: 'In your sight the whole world is like a grain of dust that tips the scales, like a drop of morning dew falling on the ground' (Wisdom 11:22-3). A grain of dust. An almost-nothing in the scale of things. A drop of dew, that disappears with the first warmth of the rising sun. But notice those four all-important words: not just a grain of dust, but a grain of dust *that tips the scales*.

The friend who exposed my 'No' spoke to me one day of his sense of wonder that, with modern technology, the entire *Encyclopaedia Britannica* can be reduced electronically almost down to a dot on a disc. He went on to say how he wished that we could see the unfolding of history, starting with the Big Bang, re-spooled in reverse. If such a thing were possible, we would be able to begin from the infinite variety of the created universe we now enjoy and inhabit, and travel backwards in time to see for ourselves its first outpouring from that primeval grain of being, smaller than 'a dot on a disc'. That, truly, was a grain of dust that tipped the scales! And surely, a grain of dust in which a loving Creator has a profound interest, since he continues, moment by moment, to hold it in being and to guide its overflow into ever-expanding space.

Words begin to fail us when we realise that in a very real and material way we ourselves were present in that Big Bang. As the astro-physicists remind us, we are made of stardust. The elements that were present in that first explosion of life are the same elements that make up our own physical being. The elements of creation, along with a spark of the very energy

Just a grain of cosmic dust,
but a grain that tips the scales

of creation, together make us who we are. Grains of dust, to be sure. But grains of dust with the potential to tip the scales and bring forth a particular revelation of the Creator's heart and mind that is ours alone to reveal.

The drop of dew tells the same story in a different way. A drop of dew is almost nothing, yet without it the growth of the earth would not happen. No water, no growth. A drop of dew, though utterly insignificant in itself, is part of earth's life support system – an essential, indispensable part. We are like drops of dew, and our lives too have the potential either to give life to all creation, or to withhold life. We give life when we allow our fleeting dewdrop to soak into the earth and water tomorrow's growth. We withhold life when we choose instead to keep our dewdrop in a little bottle for ourselves, refusing to let it be spent, refusing to let it flow.

The Kingdom journey is a call to become grains of dust that tip the scales *in favour of Life*. We know that our lives fall short of this calling in so many ways, and that all too often our choices and reactions tend to tip the scales in a direction that is *life-denying*. Before we can set out with the Lord upon the road to the Kingdom, we need to pass through the tunnel of our own deep darkness, and the deceptions and distortions that are built into the very fabric of our society. The passage through this tunnel is daunting. We proceed blindly, feeling our way forward, and helpless to find our own way back to the Light. But deep within us we hold the agate stone, the pearl of great price, the true picture in its true colours that God has seen in us beneath the fig tree. We go forward, knowing that we are *known* by God in all our brokenness, and that we are also *loved* beyond measure, and trusting that to be wholly loved is even more awesome than to be wholly known.

2. A WALK ON THE DARK SIDE

A friend of mine is pregnant, after several heartbreaking miscarriages. She has just had her first scan, and she told me of her joy at seeing a tiny heart beating inside her. That joy is still wrapped up in a tide of nausea, which accompanies the early weeks of pregnancy. She knows the fragility of the new life that she is carrying with so much love, and she knows that it will not come to birth without a great deal of pain. Yet the heart of the matter is the joy, not the sickness, or the anxiety, or the suffering.

Perhaps God feels like that about his hidden life conceived within each of us. Only he can see that tiny heart beating. We feel the sickness and the fear and the uncertainty. He listens to the little heartbeat and rejoices. It is our true self that is growing deep in our hearts. And that 'true self' is an indispensable part of the wholeness of his Kingdom, intimately inter-related with every other 'true self' growing secretly in the core of every other creature. It has the beauty of the agate stone, only seen when the stone is sliced open and polished. Or of the pearl forming inside an oyster shell, but brought into being by the presence of a painful irritant in the tender flesh of the oyster.

However we visualise it, this treasure has to do with the unique fragment of God's Being and Nature which is ours alone to reveal. The coming of the Kingdom, for which we pray daily, seems to be intimately connected with the revealing of this pure fragment of Godself in the core of each of his creatures. Yet this revealing seems to go hand in hand with a painful process of stripping, breaking and letting go of all that is blocking the emergence of truth in our own lives and in the life of all creation.

We turn now to face some of the implications of that process in the full confidence that the pain involved in this 'coming to birth' is wrapped in love. God's way of dealing with the encrustations and distortions of sin and evil that come between us and our true selves may cause us much pain, but it will lead to life. It cannot be bypassed, any more than the weeks of morning sickness or the agony in the labour ward can be bypassed in the process of bringing new life to birth. There are deep roots of untruth within us, but the heart of the matter is life not death, joy not suffering. We are not being beaten by the lashes of God's anger, but led on the reins of God's love.

The slaughter of the first-born

I remember the day when I finally got over my horror that the God, whom I regarded as a loving Father, was the same God who slaughtered the first-born of every Egyptian family at the time of the great plagues (Exodus 11:4-7). For years this kind of discrepancy had troubled me. Yet deep down I sensed that this image of a ruthless destroyer of the first-born had something to say to me personally.

The breakthrough came when I realised that I had my own variants of the 'first-born of the Egyptians'. There was a good deal wrong with my way of life, my values and attitudes and actions. They were like weeds springing up all over the garden. Cutting their heads off every so often in an honest examination of conscience was fine as far as it went, but it never seemed to get to the roots of things. It wasn't very effective, simply to offer God, however humbly, a list of my week's malices and misdemeanours, because the same things were certainly going to come back to haunt me next week. The truth was that I was making no progress at all in eradicating the destructive patterns of behaviour from my life.

It began to dawn on me that for me the 'first-born of the Egyptians' represented the roots of my own sinful attitudes. These fundamentally distorted attitudes were like 'families' or clusters of sinfulness, and the only way to eradicate them was for God to pull up the roots. He would have to destroy the *origins* of each sinful tendency and stop it spreading its seed all through my life. If the 'first-born', the real root of each destructive tendency in me, could be killed, then the 'family tree' of that particular line of sinfulness would be aborted.

I wish I could say that thereafter I let God do what I could now see that he needed to do. No! I found all kinds of ways to prevent him, and my garden is still full of weeds. However, my encounter with at least some of the roots of sin in my own life may be worth exploring and sharing, because some of these tendencies are, I suspect, common to us all. More than that, perhaps, they are endemic in our social structures and our whole way of being human.

The power of this exercise lies in its ability to reveal the deeper roots of what is going wrong in our personal lives and in the life of all creation. Such recognition may be our first step to acknowledging and 'owning' these tendencies, and choosing whether or not we want to remain enslaved to them.

The remainder of this chapter invites you to take your own 'walk on the dark side' by looking at some of the ingrained tendencies that are constantly seducing us into ever deeper confusion and alienation. In particular, we might spend a little time reflecting on:

- our ability to deceive ourselves into living as if we were self-sufficient islands and the distorted perspectives that result from this illusion;
- our willingness to use violence of all kinds to defend our illusions;
- the compulsive habits with which we maintain our securities and fill our essential emptiness.

When we have begun to recognise how these destructive patterns are operating in our own hearts, we move on to reflect on how these same patterns pervade all creation. We face honestly the dreadful possibility that, without God's grace, they are set to become the permanent reality of the way things are – a permanence to which we would have to give the name 'hell'.

The island illusion

The island illusion is perhaps the mother and father of our self-deception. It seduces us into believing ourselves to be self-sufficient, distorts our perspective and persuades us to build our lives on shifting sands.

We all know that the world consists of oceans, continents and islands. This reality is there for everyone to see. We are much less likely to stop and reflect that underneath the fluctuating water levels the world is actually just one single lump of rock, spinning through space. The continents and islands are, from this point of view, just pimples on the surface of our lump of rock. So why do they dominate our attention so?

Well, an obvious reason is that they are where we live. They contribute very significantly to making up our 'identity'. They define our culture, our language, our perception of the natural world, our eating habits and to a large (though decreasing) extent, our genetic makeup and physical attributes. If the tide were to go out, figuratively speaking, then we would lose this misleading and incomplete sense of our identity, and with it the (false) feeling of security it gives us. Not really surprising, then, that we attach more importance to our island independence than to the oneness of the bedrock below the tide-line.

*Below the tideline of our
island kingdoms ~
a bedrock wholeness*

The more I ponder this fact, the more it seems to me to reflect the way our minds and hearts function too. We see ourselves as discrete entities, autonomous and primarily responsible to ourselves. Our ability to survive, physically and emotionally, depends, so we believe, on our keeping our 'island world' in good order, and we are usually content to maintain communications with our neighbouring 'islands', as it were, above the surface. Sometimes, of course, these inter-island relations are far from good, and we wage war on each other or freeze each other into isolation.

Whether good or bad, our inter-island relationships remain superficial, if they lose sight of the bedrock underneath the 'waters' that divide us. The centre of gravity remains in the 'island', which becomes and remains the most important thing dominating our consciousness. The reality is very different, as we would instantly see if the water were all to disappear. Then we would see the earth for what it truly is – a single rock. In the same way, if the tide of consciousness were to go out (as perhaps it does after death) we would realise that in the core of our being *we are all one*. Our true and personal identity is also a part of a greater whole that still lies beyond our imagination.

Such a realisation changes things dramatically. If we are, in the heart of our being, 'all one', then anything any one of us does will potentially affect all. We are no longer primarily responsible to ourselves. We become primarily responsible to the Whole. The centre of gravity has shifted from our own island-existence to the heart of the bedrock oneness. Perhaps this is part of what Jesus means when he urges us to 'love one another'. I suggest that it is a call to relate to one another as we truly are, fellow cells in the Body of Christ, with our centre of gravity in the Whole rather than in our own little part of it.

Twenty-first century science is in some ways ahead of theology in furthering our understanding of ourselves as interrelating cells of an organic Whole. Particle physics reveals that the entire universe, as we currently understand it, is *relational*, with every particle interconnected and interrelating with every other. Biologists tell us that we exist within a web of interconnected systems, each of which affects the others. We learn that we inhabit a universe where one minor incident in one part of the Whole can have unpredictable consequences quite elsewhere.

From the perspective of our own 'island', we are easily seduced into the belief that our own preoccupations are of greater significance than anything else happening in the world around us. But the truth is that our lives are grounded on an illusion – the mistaken assumption that the 'island' is the reality and that the largely invisible 'bedrock' of our being can safely be sidelined and ignored.

The next stage down the sinful spiral is to make the rest of the world fit our false assumptions! When we start to do this – and I would suggest that there is no one alive who is not engaged in this process to some extent – then we are on the road to breakdown in all kinds of ways.

Imagine yourself as one of a family. One person in that family does something wrong, and is caught, and publicly shamed. Maybe something of this nature has happened in your own family. Meet the people involved. Let each of them tell you how the incident has affected them. The whole family, however innocent, is blighted by the one person's wrongdoing, and shares in the shame. One sinner infects the whole family. But so does one saint! How does this make you feel?

The chicken or the egg?

What actually happens, when a single cell within the Body declares itself independent? It will, so it decides, live a life of its own. The basic core program that we noticed in Chapter 1, identifying that cell with the whole of which it is a part, and identifying the unique role of that cell within the whole, is infiltrated by what, in computer terms, we might call a 'virus'. This virus tells us these two lies:

- Your inner program that identifies you with the Whole of which you are a part is meaningless. *Because you are the whole.* You are your own centre of gravity.
- Since you are all that matters, your unique role in life is to look after yourself, defend and expand yourself and arrange for the rest of creation to serve you.

The language may seem stark, but there is enough truth in it to make us pause for thought. As I look back over the events of even the last few days, I can invariably find traces of this kind of thinking. I have almost certainly made choices based upon exactly this rationale. The deep truth at the core of my being has been infiltrated by this subtle virus of untruth that tries to convince me:

- that my illusion of autonomy is the reality, and
- that the reality of the bedrock one-ness of all creation, and my own co-responsibility for the health of that Whole is an illusion.

The virus turns reality upside down and inside out. Our minds and hearts are pitched into confusion.

One way that helps me grasp what is happening in this confusion is to think of that deep core of my being as my 'true self' and to realise that a false self – I could call it my 'ego-self' – is building up around that true self, sometimes threatening to choke it completely. The 'ego-self' colludes with all the false programming that tells me that the most important item is 'me' and my role is to nourish, defend and expand that 'me', even at the expense of the rest of creation.

I remember being quite amazed to learn that the problem with cancerous cells is that their 'die' program doesn't work. Healthy cells, apparently, know when to die, in order to maintain the health and viability of the whole body. Cancerous cells have lost this ability and so keep on multiplying, until they take over the whole organism. My ego-self seems a bit like that. All it knows is how to grow and expand, eating away insatiably at everything around, but it doesn't know when enough is enough! A bit like an eggshell that thinks it is the main thing about the egg, and loses sight entirely of the fact that the egg is there to carry the embryonic chick.

My ego-self has a very necessary and positive role to play: it is there to hold and protect my embryonic 'true self', but it also lives constantly at risk of losing sight of this reality and becoming wholly absorbed in its own kingdom. It tends to resist, with all its force, the requirement to let go and disintegrate, when the time comes, like an eggshell, to let the chick of my true self hatch into eternal life. My true self, my inner chick, therefore may have to force its way out by breaking the shell, or else die without ever seeing the light of eternity. There is a conflict being waged between life and death, even in the tiniest cell of my body and in every movement of my heart.

My ego-self's adamant refusal to 'die' causes it to throw the whole of me into a diseased state. Instead of letting go, like an outgrown skin, when the time is ripe, it multiplies wildly. The result is a much more far-reaching kind of death that affects all creation.

Like the grain of wheat, of which Jesus speaks (in John 12:24), eventually our ego-selves will also fall into the ground, and into apparent disintegration, but the result will be the eternal liberation of our true selves, to grow and bear fruit that will last.

Imagine a doctor diagnosing you as a cancerous cell in the Body of Christ. How do you feel? Let the doctor take your medical history, in order to determine what gave rise to the cancer. Look, in prayer, at the cultural, social and personal issues that gave rise to it. The doctor offers to heal you, but this will mean surrendering your whole being to him, body and mind. How will you choose? Which is more important to you – your independence, or the health of the whole Body?

The killer within

The road to breakdown twists round the next deadly bend as soon as our island autonomy is challenged. What happens when our personal island interests clash with those of someone else? The book of Genesis gives us a graphic answer to this question, in the story of Cain and Abel. These two brothers are the products of a 'fallen world'. They have already been infected by the virus of autonomy. They are living the island illusion.

Abel is a shepherd. Cain is a farmer. The time comes for the two to make their thank-offering to God. Abel brings a lamb. Cain brings some of the produce of the fields. At this point, however, things go wrong. For whatever reason, Cain believes that his offering to God has not been as well received as Abel's. He becomes jealous of his brother's perceived higher standing with God. The fact that this perception is mistaken, and is actually just another manifestation of the distorted perspective we get on things when we live in our island worlds, doesn't enter into his reasoning.

Rivalry leads to jealousy. Jealousy hardens into embittered envy. Envy festers into hate. Hate leads to murder. The downward spiral is unstoppable. Cain has been taken over by it and the consequences are inevitable. Soon Abel lies in a pool of blood and Cain flees in panic, to be pursued for ever by the voice of God: 'Your brother's blood is crying out to me from the ground. Now be cursed and banned from the ground that has opened its mouth to receive your brother's blood at your hands.'

The immediacy and the relevance of this dreadful sentence comes home to us every day. The blood of Abel cries out from every land on earth and from our own city streets. It screams at us from every newspaper. And it flows from the same deadly spiral:

- A threat to our personal sovereignty and imagined security makes us defensive.

- This defensive fear (of losing our identity and security) makes us envy the perceived advantages of others.
- The overwhelming force of this envy and jealousy blots out all claims of reason and humanity and leads us to do violence.

The violent reaction can take many forms. Do you recognise any of these possibilities in your own reactions?

- We can get rid of the threat by eliminating the person who embodies it, as Cain did to Abel. Most of us won't commit murder in our lifetime, but just as surely most of us *will* freeze someone out of our landscape, or 'cut someone dead' or propagate a lie about them in order to undermine their reputation (and thereby boost our own!). We may never kill with our own hands, but we collude every day with violence perpetrated in our name in all kinds of subtle ways by our own democratically elected governments and other (including religious) institutions, against those whose existence is perceived to be a threat to our collective security.
- Often, however, the bad feelings that are threatening to us, have their origins in our own hearts. What then? We don't want to eliminate ourselves, so we project the bad feeling onto someone else, or onto a whole group of 'others'. We pile the problem onto the back of a scapegoat. We engage in the 'blame chain', with scant regard for the truth of the matter. It may begin with playground bullying and it can lead all the way to Auschwitz.
- A third violent reaction is to seize for ourselves what we envy in another. Most of us would loudly condemn material theft, but which of us has never mortgaged our time and energy in order to possess material benefits that we have envied in others? The bigger house, the newer car, the foreign holiday? Perhaps we only damaged ourselves in the process, winding ourselves up into a state of hyperactivity for the sake of a fleeting pleasure. But usually others will also have been affected – our family, our friends, our colleagues, our little children who have been robbed of the quality time they had the right to expect of us.

Violence is good at disguising itself. We can even 'kill with kindness' when our determination to feel good about ourselves tempts us to snuff out another person's self-respect by forcing our 'helpfulness' upon them, unbidden, unneeded and unwanted.

The same dynamic – of gaining our own advantage at the expense of others – seems to lie behind every world war and every family quarrel. Whichever way we turn, we feel helpless to free ourselves from its all-entangling web.

Read the story of Cain and Abel in Genesis 4:1-16, letting yourself be imaginatively present to the action. Have your own fears and compulsions ever spiralled down into acts of violence, either physical, verbal or emotional, in thought or in deed, or have you ever been the victim of another's violence? Without judging either yourself or anyone else, let this destructive pattern lie open before God in your prayer and beg him for healing and for genuine enlightenment about the origins of these feelings and thoughts or actions.

Captives of compulsion

Another question that looms, once we have committed ourselves to building our lives on the illusion of island independence is this: What do we have to do – and keep on doing – in order to *maintain* our (false) position?

We have looked at some of the ways in which we commonly *defend* it against threat or attack. But even when there is no attack or threat, we find, very quickly, that our island illusion has a voracious appetite. Just as trying to maintain a physical position that isn't natural to us will cost us a huge effort and a lot of pain, so too it will cost us dearly to maintain our false position of supposed autonomy.

If we look at some common human behaviour patterns, several maintenance strategies become apparent:

- We can surround ourselves with defence systems. We may avoid intimacy in relationships, lest anyone come close enough to challenge us. At work we may fall into a compulsive habit of 'covering our backs' in order to prove ourselves on some point, or incriminate someone else.
- We can use all kinds of lesser goods to fill the emptiness inside us. We sense that we have lost something infinitely precious in becoming an 'island'. We may feel that this lost 'wholeness' would be found in perfect love, if only we could discover it. We fill the inner void, perhaps quite literally, with chocolate or cigarettes. We anaesthetise ourselves against

the inner pain, with alcohol or drugs, compulsive work or casual sex, or with compulsive shopping, which has become so common that we have coined a new term for it: 'retail therapy'.

- More subtly, we can collude with everyone else's island illusion, bolstering them in their separateness so as to keep them at a safe distance from our own. In this way we construct mutual admiration (or ego-boosting) societies and keep our self-esteem mutually groomed. False friendships are made of this, and so is many an 'old boys' network'.
- We can appease all potential aggressors, in pursuit of a quiet life. This 'peace at any price' strategy can be as destructive, in its own way, as outright violence, blocking out all challenges to the status quo and inhibiting the possibility of genuine growth back into wholeness.

Once enmeshed in these compulsive tendencies, we are in real danger of re-arranging creation to fit our false assumptions. Indeed, history itself gets rewritten to turn inconvenient truth into more palatable untruth. The speed at which we can then be sucked into the downward spiral of destruction is truly frightening. Compulsion is a cumulative process, feeding upon itself, and insatiable in its demands. The Old Testament story of David and Bathsheba is a powerful portrayal of this terrible process.

David looks out one day over the surrounding houses, and sees the beautiful Bathsheba bathing, in what she believes is privacy.

The downward spiral begins with David's desire for her. He acts on this desire. He sends for her. He seduces her and makes her pregnant.

Once the fact of the coming child is discovered, the situation becomes darker than mere dalliance. This is an unexpected problem. The facts must be re-arranged to make it look as though Bathsheba's lawful husband, Uriah, is the father of her child. But this same lawful husband is a soldier, fighting David's wars, far away from his wife's bed.

David's solution to this difficulty is to recall Uriah from the wars on the pretence of giving him some recreational leave. Whatever happens, David must make sure that Uriah sleeps with Bathsheba during this leave, so that the breach in David's defences can be closed. But Uriah has no such intention. In spite of David's attempts to make him drunk and get him carted off home, Uriah remains obdurately 'on duty' at the palace.

Thus thwarted, David has to look for stronger measures to ensure his own safety. He arranges for Uriah to be sent back to battle and placed deliberately on the front line, where he will certainly be killed. In this way the threat to David's personal 'kingdom' is permanently eliminated, and the road ahead, with Bathsheba, is cleared. The satisfaction of his compulsion has led David through the labyrinths of lust and deception into pre-meditated murder.

It would be easier to cope with this grim story if David were more obviously a 'bad guy'. Unfortunately he is everyone's idea of a 'nice young man'. He is the same David who fought and overcame Goliath, tended the sheep on the hillsides and composed many of the psalms. The same David, youngest and least likely of the sons of Jesse, who was chosen by God to be anointed with the spirit of Yahweh.

In short, David is just like one of us. Fundamentally decent. And funda-mentally flawed! Like David, we are all caught up in a chain reaction. And the chain that we are forging imprisons us in our own compulsions – individual and collective. Let there indeed be shame, for our part in this mess – a sense of shame that at last can shake us free from the opiate of denial. And let there be confusion, that acknowledges our total helplessness to redeem ourselves. From these two reactions God can weave something new.

The story of David's descent into depravity has a sequel. Nathan the prophet chal-lenges him, with the story of the poor man whose one ewe lamb was stolen. When David flies into a rage about this injustice, Nathan makes him stop and reflect on his own behaviour. 'You are that man,' he tells him. The words turn David's life round and set him back on the road to wholeness.

Read the story of David (2 Samuel 11:1-17 and 12:1-15) for yourself, and try to enter into it imaginatively. Where do you find yourself in this story? Have you any memories of being sucked down into a spiral of ever-increasing untruth and wrong action, in which each false step seemed to lead to something worse? If so, just bring it to God now in your prayer and ask him to show you its first roots and the extent of its consequences. Listen to the reproach of Nathan. How will you choose to respond?

A cascade of sin

So far we have been focusing for the most part on the effects of our own sinful tendencies. And indeed, 'ourselves' are the only thing we can change. However, these same tendencies are evident in the whole of creation, and for this reason we need to reflect on the larger picture, so that we may gain a truer perspective on our own place within it.

The sin of the angels

One evening I watched a video reconstructing the first few moments following the Big Bang, and learned, with great interest, that in the beginning of creation there were almost equal numbers of particles and anti-particles. Without needing to worry about what exactly are 'particles' and 'anti-particles', what gripped me in this fact was that the two are mutually destructive, cancelling each other out. One could say, more poetically, that there was a physical struggle between life and death, between light and darkness, between plus and minus.

As I watched, I recalled other representations of a primeval struggle. I had read many poems and plays about just such a struggle. And I had been taught about the fall of the angels, and the casting of the dark spirits into the depths of hell. I had perhaps regarded these stories as mythical fantasies. Yet here was a scientific video telling me a very similar story. I began to wonder whether our human psyche is not, after all, carrying the imprinted memory of a real, elemental confrontation, played out in the heart of creation, between what leads to life and what spirals down into non-existence.

What led to life, in the creation story, among many other factors, was that there was a tiny imbalance between the quantity of particles as against anti-particles. The difference was minute (measured by particle physicists as the ninth decimal place of one per cent). When I learned this, my heart leapt! I knew that I had stumbled upon God's 'preferential option for Life'. The struggle of 'the angels' has been definitively won by the forces of Light and Life. Creation spells it out for us. Were it not so, there would have been no physical creation at all, because the matter, from which our physical being and all that supports it, derives would have been entirely destroyed by the anti-matter.

The sin of Adam and Eve

If creation displays a picture of the first round of the struggle between life and death, the next stage is expressed, biblically, in the story of Adam and Eve in the Garden of Eden (and in similar stories in other religions and cultures). The human psyche, it appears, has a deep, unconscious awareness, of a crucial, and fatal, desire to grasp at independence and autonomy. In the drama of Eden, we see the effects of sin on our human societies and in our personal and social relationships. Let's take a look at what was going on in Eden, and at the dynamic that pitched us into disaster.

We might identify these stages in the process of losing touch with God and, as we do so, we might reflect on how far these movements are present in our own lives too:

- First the desire for autonomy arises. In Eden it is suggested by the serpent. In terms of the 'island and the bedrock', the serpent suggests something like: 'You don't have to buy into the bedrock Wholeness. You can choose to let your own little island become the whole reality. On your own island you can be the unchallenged ruler. You can arrange things as you wish, to keep yourself happy and in control.'

- When it is apparently too late to reverse the decision, our first parents realise that the 'island kingdom' they have chosen is pathetically small, and is isolated from the day-to-day communion with creation, and its creator, that they had once enjoyed. They have turned away from the Light – the source of their being and they are looking into their own shadow. This is what is meant by the state of 'spiritual desolation', in which we focus our attention upon ourselves, and eventually see only our own long dark shadow looming ahead of us. In this darkness, quite obviously, we cannot see each other any more, and our island isolation is intensified.

- By their own choice, they have alienated themselves from the Wholeness represented by the picture of the garden. Their banishment from paradise is the inevitable outcome of their own choice, and not some arbitrary act of revenge by a frustrated 'god'. Their pain, on realising what they have lost, is projected outwards, in a 'blame chain'. Adam blames Eve, and Eve blames the serpent for the consequences of their choice. Blame is a symptom of denial. 'This can't possibly be my fault. If I acknowledge that it is my own fault, then I am admitting that I got it all wrong, and my life is built on the wrong foundation.'

- The sentence seems hard. First a life of hard labour, and then, death. Is this just a punishment? Or is it something that ultimately holds the promise of a new life? The sentence to wrest their living from a reluctant earth is also the call to be co-creators, to labour with God once more to bring his

Kingdom to being in his creation. The pronouncement of an inevitable physical death is also an act of protective love, limiting the effects of the Fall to time and space and preventing them from becoming eternal.

Finally, in a most touching vignette, the author of Genesis offers us a picture of God making tunics for his fallen children, from animal skins. Out of the broken strands of his Dream for creation, God, we discover, picks up the pieces, and continues to weave the Dream. We shall see, in the next stage of our journey, how there is a sequel to this weaving, as humankind is called into direct partnership with God to restore the lost Wholeness. God sets about recreating the Kingdom of Life, by weaving a web of love and restored relationship.

Read the story of Adam and Eve (Genesis 1–3). Imagine yourself present at the very beginning of creation. In what ways are you aware of being in touch with the 'wholeness' of creation (perhaps in a truly loving relationship, or in your feelings for the natural world, or your concern for other people or other species)? In what ways do you feel cut off and isolated in your own 'island kingdom'? Look back over the past few days. When have you made decisions and taken action that served your own 'kingdom' at the expense of the larger world? How do you feel about what you find?

The sin of you and me

And so the cascade of sin comes brimming down the cliff-sides of creation, to drown you and me in its lethal torrent. Every multi-national corporation, every limited company, every parish council and every family home is affected by the virus. The cascade of deception and illusion affects everything we do as individuals, and our individual choices and actions, likewise made from a state of self-deception and delusion, affect the whole of creation. One dysfunctional cell affects the whole body. A dysfunction in any part of the body ultimately affects every cell.

Let us ask ourselves, personally, a few of the questions that reverberate through the pages of Genesis:

- In what specific ways have I chosen 'my kingdom' during the past few days, and put out of my mind the possible effects of my choice on others? How far has my tendency to choose in this way become habitual?

- Am I actually living all my conscious life on the island of my own kingdom? Have I already lost my awareness of the bedrock Wholeness underlying creation? Do I really listen to, and empathise with, other people? How willing am I to 'lose myself' when I am engaged with another person's story, or engrossed in the wonder of the created world?

- Do I tend to shift the blame for my faults? Am I in denial? Look back honestly over the past few days. Have you employed the 'blame chain' at all? Can you see what you were actually hiding from, in doing so? You might find it helpful, though mortifying, to ask someone close to you to enlighten you on this. One of the worst effects of our sin is the blindness that comes with it. In the darkness of sin we can't even see what we are up to!

What scapegoats are tethered
to the end of your 'blame chains'?

When I reflect on the scale of the problem in this way, I begin to move towards a more realistic sense of the deep and crying need for healing. Alone, so it seems, I can do nothing to get free of the web of deception that grips creation. Yet if I do not do what I alone *can* do, the universal breakdown cannot be halted, let alone reversed. 'Hell', it might seem, is not just a word to be cast lightly into conversation, but potentially a state of alienation into which the whole of creation could slide.

At a time when you are alone in the house, after nightfall, put out all the lights, close your eyes, and try to make your way from one room to another. Notice the feelings of helplessness as you grope your way forward, slowly feeling for familiar objects that you can no longer see. You have lost your points of reference. You are blind. How do you feel? Inwardly, we are all groping our way through life in this kind of darkness, unable to see the true self of each other, unable to trust the landscape on which we are forced to rely. If you can do so safely, light a candle now in the darkness of your home, and bring your inner blindness to God, begging him to rekindle his Light within you.

Hell – a myth, or a real possibility?

Does the concept of 'hell' have any meaning for us today, now that the notion of a physical place of torment has been largely consigned to history?

It may well feel like 'hell' on the motorway in the rush hour, or when our teenagers are blasting the house with decibels. But perhaps we come closer to a sense of 'hell' when we reflect on what, if anything, has made us say that a personal experience 'felt like hell'.

When have you used the word 'hell' recently, and really *meant* it? In what context did you say it? What feelings and circumstances gave rise to your sense of touching 'hell'?

The answers will be different for everyone, of course. But the following states of mind might ring some bells:

- Feelings of being caught in a web of demands and compulsions and 'torn in all directions'.
- Burning with a desire that can't be satisfied or eaten up with a longing that can never be fulfilled.
- Feeling drowned in an emptiness inside that feels like a cave of aching for something

we may not even be able to name – the kind of emptiness we habitually fill with 'busy-ness'.

- Wading through treacle, or pushing a stone uphill, only to watch it roll down again, over and over, day after day.
- Feeling enslaved to our own worst fears, especially the fear that we might lose what we have become dependent on.
- Feeling paralysed, frozen into someone else's 'kingdom', or overwhelmed with baggage too heavy to bear.
- Fear that deep down we have no 'identity' except what we construct by acquiring status or possessions.
- Fear that when we die no one will notice the difference.

One key, perhaps, to gaining a sense of what 'hell' means for us, lies in discovering that when we have gained our 'independence' there is a big hollow inside us – the hollow left behind where the bedrock wholeness used to be. It is the ache we cannot fill, the absence of what we most long for.

Instinctively we will try to fill that void with lesser things. And this will seduce us into the hell of idolatry. We will almost certainly, at some stage in our lives, project our deepest longings onto another human being. This tendency can get all mixed up with the feeling of 'being in love'. It turns into 'hell' (for ourselves and for the other person), when we subconsciously desire and expect that person to fill the deep void within us. No one can ever do that. Human lives are just not that big! To ask of another that they fill our deepest void is to suck them down into our own personal hell. And when they fail, as fail they must, or when they refuse, as refuse they should, the 'love' will so easily turn to anger and to hate.

Reflect on the shape of your own deepest personal emptiness and aching. Have you tried to ask others to fill it? If so, just bring this insight into prayer. And because this process is always unconscious, ask for God's enlightenment to reveal any places of compulsion in your living.

This is a demanding exercise, and may cause a lot of pain. An example may help. Let's join a fictitious young man called Jamie. Jamie has had a brutal childhood. His father was in prison for much of the time, and when he was home, he was cruel and insensitive. As a young man Jamie gets involved with the church. The pastor, Gary, takes a lot of trouble to help Jamie, and Jamie rapidly becomes attached to him, and dependent. He projects onto Gary all the aching void that he could name 'absent father'. Deep down, he convinces himself that Gary can fill this void. Eventually Gary is moved on, and leaves the district. Jamie loses control and attacks Gary. In his anger and his grief he breaks the contact with his friends in the church. The downward spiral takes him rapidly into a life on the streets, where he transfers his dependence on Gary into a dependence on heroin. He has slipped into hell.

The patterns of self-deception, of violence and of compulsion have the potential to become our eternal reality if we so choose. This is not the threat of a manipulative medieval religious system, but a possibility that lives in the depths of our own being. To choose to let God free us from the chain reaction that leads to this permanent alienation from life itself is not a matter of merely repeating creeds or assenting to doctrines. It requires a radical reappraisal of ourselves and of the structures of our society and a willingness to allow these to be transformed by the values of the gospel. This is the challenge of the journey that lies ahead of us.

The call of life

If we had to give a name to the archenemy of life, we might call it 'fear' – of loneliness, of isolation, of rejection, of emptiness, of meaninglessness and non-existence. Fear makes us into cowards and bullies, doormats and tyrants, perpetrators and colluders in the inherent evils of our systems.

Yet Jesus constantly assures us that perfect love casts out fear. Fear and love remind me of the primeval struggle between matter and anti-matter. They are mutually destructive. Fear undermines and destroys real love, but love casts out fear. The journey with the Lord is a journey into love. The same Love that knows the beauty locked up inside the agate stone, and the pearl growing within the oyster. It is the story of God's continuing option for Life. We are called to be Easter People – pilgrims in hope, not in despair, travelling into Life not death. Love always has the edge over fear. The margin may be small, but God's preferential option is always for Love.

Our encounter with the darkness within us must leave us humbled, yet also with a true sense of wonder. The wonder is that in all this mayhem, in which reality itself has been utterly distorted and overturned – in ourselves, in our relationships, in all our human society and in the cosmos itself – in all of this we not only survive, but *grow*.

Trapped in our own defences;
reduced to shadows
of who we could be

Imagine yourself as having survived a potentially terminal illness. The doctors have just told you that all is well, and you can expect a normal life. What do you want to do? Are there any parts of your life that you would like to change, given such an opportunity? Or imagine yourself as having been forgiven by a friend you have deeply hurt. What do you want to say to that friend? Given a chance to start again, what would you want to change in your relationship with that friend?

Life itself is on our side. And it calls us, in God's name, to be people who are on the side of Life. In this spirit, therefore, we move on to experience God's call to be partners with him in the great enterprise of Life.

3. THE KINGDOM VENTURE

It would be good to feel that now we have come through Chapter 2, we have successfully negotiated the 'tunnel of darkness'. Jesus, we might hope, stands at the other end, waiting to welcome us into the rest of our journey with him. While in one sense this is true, at a deeper level such a picture would be another distortion of the truth. A truer picture might be that we have summoned (or been given) the courage to face the darkness within us, and allow God to shed his light upon it. And now Jesus has, amazingly (in view of our track record!), called us to walk with him, learning from him new ways of bringing his light into our own lives and the lives of others. This call, to be his companions and his co-workers in the revealing of God's Kingdom on earth, is not a reward for good behaviour in Chapter 2. It is a call to open up our particular darkness to become a place where a bit more of the redemption story can proceed, so that the darkness may be lightened a little more, for the sake of all creation. It is a call, freely to choose to make a living journey that reveals, and enables, life in its fullest form.

We begin by remembering that we are indeed entangled in a web of untruth, deception and delusion. Our faulty perspective still, for the most part, blinds us to the demands of justice, love and peace, making us put 'me' first in almost everything we do. If you look back over a typical day you will find countless examples of when this has been the case. When we reflect on these facts, we can so easily fall into despair, in the face of the impossibility of disentangling ourselves.

A certain mood of despair, though a far less serious one, was around in my own life one July. We had just moved into a newly built house. The 'garden' was still wild woodland, with an awkward steep drop halfway down, where in some distant age a bulldozer had excavated the hill we lived on. We had co-existed with this wilderness for quite a while, and it was clear, from their body language, that our neighbours thought it was high time we fixed it. To 'fix it', however, required either money we didn't have, or energy we couldn't (or wouldn't) spare. The situation was getting mildly desperate. The 'garden' was growing over our heads.

Eventually a friend offered to bring his mechanical digger to work on it. The result was astounding. In the course of just one day, the wilderness was neatly stepped and layered, and the entire population of weeds and brambles disappeared. The newly reclaimed garden was going to require our ongoing attention, but the task had become one that we could at least co-operate with.

Now, as I recall this problem with the garden, and how it was resolved, I begin to catch the first glimmerings of understanding as to how creation's redemption story proceeds.

A two-pronged fork

The 'garden', you recall, was completely wild. It wasn't a garden at all. We had sat and stared at it with ever-increasing dismay, day after day. Between the magnitude of the task, and our own lack of direction and energy, it was beginning to look like a hopeless cause. Like creation itself, it was a tangle of competing growths, each vying for its own place in the 'kingdom' and fighting for the space and light that was available. It was a riot of confusion, in which it had become impossible to get 'to the roots' of the problems. We were ashamed of it – and we had every reason to be so!

The solution to the problem had two components. It needed a decisive intervention with the help of the mechanical digger, and an ongoing commitment to tend and cherish the land from then on. We couldn't even begin without the decisive intervention, but without our ongoing commitment to work the land, the intervention of the digger would have been to no avail. From the very beginning, there was a call to co-operation.

This story helps me to get in touch with the beginning of the redemption story of all creation, through the incarnation of Jesus. It helps me to recognise that two lines of approach are called for: one from God, the other from ourselves.

The destitution of our sin and our brokenness requires decisive action. Something needs to happen to fish us out of the quicksands. We might usefully picture this 'something' as a two-pronged fork.

The first prong is God's initiative. With the best, and most determined will in the world, our own desire to co-operate will not come anywhere near what is needed to make creation whole again. For this to happen, God will make his own decisive intervention in the human story, to the extent of becoming fully embodied within it, with all that this implies, as we will explore in Chapter 4.

The other prong is our own desire to be lifted out of the quicksands and to co-operate in whatever way we can with our own rescue and the restoration of all creation to its original wholeness. For God's intervention to be effective, an ongoing commitment is needed from us, to 'work the land', to live our lives in ways that allow the incarnate God to redeem every aspect of human fallenness. In this chapter we reflect on the personal call to be part of this Kingdom Venture. The decision about how we respond to this call is ours alone to make – our privilege and our responsibility.

God's decisive intervention
asks for our
ongoing commitment

In our garden problem we faced two fundamental questions:

- Do we actually *want* this land to become a garden or not?
- If so, are we prepared to consent to, and co-operate with whatever has to be done to let the land be redeemed?

At this point in our Kingdom journey, too, we face a fundamental question. Do we really *want* to walk this Way? Do we *really* want the original wholeness of our being and of the being of all creation to be restored? If so, are we willing to allow that restoration to happen, *whatever the cost*? These are not disabling questions, to undermine our confidence. They are questions that invite us to explore the deeper reaches of our desiring.

Our search for our own authentic answer to this question will require us to dig deep into our personal experience, allowing God's love to make it fruitful in ways still beyond our imagination. It is a search for the bedrock of our being. And the more we dig, the more insistently we are confronted by the question:

Where *is* the ground of our being? Where is the *solid* ground?

The Bottom Line

In view of the deep-rooted untruth and self-deception we uncovered in Chapter 2, we might feel we have lost all sense of solid ground beneath our feet. Few of us have any job security any more, and, increasingly, we are unable to rely on the permanence of our committed relationships. Everything within us and around us is potentially untrustworthy – our own motives, the structures of our social, political and religious institutions, our own story and the world's story. We have built our lives on shifting sand. We have made life-changing decisions on the basis of wrong data. And to cover our tracks, we have rewritten history to conceal our mistakes. We have even tried to rearrange creation, in all manner of ways, to fit in with our own illusions.

One of Jesus' best-known parables opens up these feelings in us and spells out the consequences of building our lives on quicksands.

Where is the ground of my being? And what are the shifting sands?

Read the story of the Prodigal Son, in Luke 15:11-31, and try to enter into it imaginatively. Imagine yourself, in turn, as each of the three people involved: the younger son, the elder son and the father. How do you feel in each of these roles? Bring to this prayer those specific sinful tendencies you have discovered in yourself. Allow yourself to turn away from the father's love and flee into the darkness and loneliness of exile. Enter your own experience of the desperation that makes you 'hit the rock' and realise that a drastic change of course is required. Then make the slow, humble journey back home and allow the father to receive you.

When the younger son realises the extent of his extremity he stares despair in the face. All his former certainties are swept away. Everything he had hoped for is lost. He has burned his boats and there is nothing left to lose. At that point, for us, as for him, there can be a radical turnaround. When there is nothing left to lose, there is everything to hope for! When we have gone as far into the pit as it is possible to go, there is only one possibility: to turn round and *return*. The rock that we hit, and that shatters us, is also the catalyst for our turning, and returning. Ironically, it is the only solid ground that is left to us, but it is solid ground indeed, as we know to our cost. It is the Bottom Line, below which there is nothing. It is the starting point for the onward journey.

When have you experienced the loss of something, or someone, you thought you couldn't possibly live without? Or perhaps the deep disappointment of failing to achieve something you had set your heart on? When has the floor opened up beneath you and let you down?

If you think back over situations like these, can you see now what 'false floors' you were trusting, as if they were the ground of your being? Recall how it felt, to discover that these things that seemed so solid, were flimsy and fragile and could not hold the weight of your reality and your life. Ask yourself:

- Where was the ground of my being in those situations?
- Where is the ground of my being now?
- Where do I want the ground of my being to be in the future?

The younger son in the story discovered that neither his father's in-heritance, nor the freedom it seemed to offer him, nor the pleasures of his uninhibited lifestyle, constituted solid ground. Paradoxically, he only rediscovered solid ground when he acknowledged his absolute destitution.

A radical turnaround

If we really desire to be participants in the Kingdom Venture, then we too face the need for radical realignment in our lives. There is a call, which will never go away, to work consciously against the 'me first' mentality which is so ingrained in our human living, and to align our hearts, instead, with the deeper centre of gravity, who is God, our only solid ground.

A decisive act of will is required to turn away from those things that are entangling us further and further into untruth, deception and delusion, and to turn in the direction of what we know, deep in the core of our being, is true. The story of the Prodigal Son illustrates just how hard this turn-around can be. This is not a once-and-for-all 'conversion' experience, crucial though such an experience may have been in our lives. It is a 'turn-ing' (or 'metanoia') that may be asked of us many times a day in our ordinary lived experience.

How do we know when we are being challenged by such a call to 'turn'? And how might we begin to respond?

Let's go back to the Prodigal Son and see what light his story sheds on our own. When I try to enter into his situation imaginatively, and prayerfully, I pick up the following clues:

- A growing awareness deep inside me that a particular direction is lead-ing me further away from what the core of my being senses to be true for me. A growing discomfort with myself. A growing sense of alienation from who I really am.
- A rock bottom experience of reaching a place from which I am helpless to escape. The feeling of having run myself into the end of a cul-de-sac.
- A resistance to admit that I have come a long way down a wrong track. Leading to a tendency to justify my wrong choices and rearrange things to fit them.
- Finally, the humiliating realisation that, after all, I can't go any further alone, and I have to ask for help.

Sometimes this experience of metanoia is big and obvious. Much more frequently it creeps up on us in small, everyday situations, or ongoing relationships that are drawing us away from our own truth.

Reflect on any areas of your own life where you sense this deep-down discomfort with the way things are going. Can you pinpoint the reasons for this unease? Can you see any build-up of a pattern of choosing to react in ways that are not really 'you' in these situations?

Have you ever felt you had reached 'the end of the cul-de-sac', and been forced to reassess yourself? If so, try reliving it in the light of prayer and ask the Lord to shed new light on that turning-point in your living. If you are in such a place now, ask the Lord to show you what is needed, to make the turning, and then be still, to listen to the stirrings of his Spirit in your depths.

Look back over the past twenty-four hours. Notice any incidents in which you felt you were acting on the impulse from movements from the deep core of your being.

Just remember how that felt, and ask God to show you how best to move forward now in the light of that sense of truth, in that particular choice or situation. Now recall any incidents where you feel you were acting on impulses that did not come from the true core of your being. If those situations are still active, can you see any way of changing the direction of your way of reacting to them?

Preparing to commit

It will cost us a real, and ongoing, effort, to act against what is pulling us into untruth. But there are some important ways in which we can help ourselves and each other.

We can spend real time alone in prayer at frequent intervals. This doesn't have to mean an hour on our knees every morning before daybreak! But it does mean making a real effort to find quality time to be alone with God. Be realistic about the time you can actually give to prayer, and try to honour that time faithfully. The more of yourself that you give to prayer, the more fruit it will bear in your life. A friend of mine expresses this as an invitation to give 'more of me, rather than more time given by less of me'. The journey that lies ahead of us in this book depends on your willingness to enter into prayer regularly, trusting that God will always meet you there and open up the next step of the way.

We can soak up the wisdom of the Word in Scripture. Consider taking a few minutes each day, perhaps to read and reflect on the daily readings, if you come from a Christian tradition that uses a common lectionary. Otherwise you might find one of the many available daily reading booklets helpful. Or simply let your heart guide you. Our journey together will frequently invite you to reflect on the scriptural accounts of Jesus' life and ministry.

We can share our journeys. Do you have a 'soul-friend'? (Also sometimes called a 'mentor' or 'spiritual companion' or, very misleadingly, a 'spiritual director'.) A soul friend is simply a companion with whom you feel able to share something of your experience of this 'Kingdom journey'. This will be someone whom you can trust absolutely and who is 'on your wavelength'. A soul friend will listen to your story, and perhaps do a little pathfinding with you. You may find it helpful to meet with such a person on a regular basis (perhaps every few weeks) to share something of where God has been for you in the intervening period. This practice gives us companionship along what can sometimes feel like a very lonely road. It also offers us a way of checking out our own experience and having another person reflect back to us where the growth points are and where the negative energies seem to be taking over. It helps us to nourish the growth, and to act against the negative pull within us.

Finally, for most people at least, there is a strong invitation to become, or remain part of a faith community, or some gathering of people who share a similar spiritual vision. For some this may be a conventional 'church', or perhaps a housegroup or any other committed group of Christians, seeking to follow the Lord together as a coherent part of the Body of Christ. For others it may be a less clearly defined grouping, perhaps a simple gathering of a few friends to share the journey with each other. But to try to make the journey of Christian discipleship in isolation is unwise, for a number of reasons:

- It exposes us to loneliness and the possibility of going off-track without realising it.
- It isn't the model that Jesus gave us. He worked with a group of committed friends and the reports we have of the early Church show that this pattern continued.
- Personal individualism is contrary to the relational nature of God himself, whom we believe to be a triune God, three Persons in one Unity. As Christians we believe that we are called to be *in relation* to God and to each other. Our relationships with other pilgrims are an important way of seeking to live out this interrelatedness.

From passive devotion to active trust

The call to be *in relation* lies very close to the heart of the 'Kingdom Venture'. A friend of mine shed some powerful light on this kind of inter-relationship recently, as he told me about his enjoyment, in younger years, of mountaineering. With his permission, I would like to share something of how this experience led him into a deeper insight about the nature of our calling to be co-creators of the Kingdom.

Imagine a lovely sunny day in a mountainous landscape. Different people feel drawn to enjoy the mountains in different ways. One loves the scenery, but needs to feel safe. He drives his car to a designated viewpoint, and parks it there, on a solid asphalt car park. He takes out his picnic lunch and sits on a bench not too far from the car, to enjoy the view. He is engaging with the mountains in his own way. We could even say that he is expressing his devotion to the natural beauty around him. He is paying it attention and appreciating it. But there is no risk involved. The car park is unlikely to be destroyed by an earthquake, and he is unlikely to lose his way back to the car at the end of the day. He is standing on one kind of solid ground. If others come, he will tolerate them, or even welcome them, but he doesn't *need* anyone else in order to engage with the mountains.

A group of climbers comes on the scene. There are three of them, carrying ropes and wearing strong boots and protective clothing. They have a different way of engaging with the mountains. They are going to climb right into them. For most of the day they will be facing stark rock faces, before they catch a glimpse of the breathtaking views from the summit. Their day will consist of hard physical graft and focused concentration. Most importantly, they will spend the day linked to each other by means of the rope. One of them will go ahead, in any particular pitch, and when he finds a good anchor point, he will fix the rope and give the signal to the next to begin the climb. At every point along the way they will remain in intimate relationship with each other. They trust each other, and they trust their ropes. This is the only basis on which they can proceed. They are, in every sense, *committing* themselves to the mountain and to each other, and that level of commitment depends on their mutual *trust*.

The Kingdom journey is more like that of the climbers than that of the man in the car park. It calls us to *engage with* the Gospel journey, and not just to gaze at it from the safety of our prayer corner. We will often feel that we are facing a rock face, and wish we could have an easier access to our heart's desire. We will discover, as we go, just what form that real commitment might take for each of us, but for now, as we set out, we need to focus on that picture of *relationship*, and the trust that it both demands and engenders. If we desire to engage deeply with the mystery of life, we must do so in relationship, and not in isolation.

In the past, scientists believed that 'creation' was like a machine, and if we could discover how each part of it works, we would understand what it is all about. Now that view has moved on, and we are learning that our whole universe is relational. It is made up of particles that are intimately interrelated with each other, forming a dynamic process of continuing

Engaging with the mountain, or just enjoying the view?

creation. A similar shift of understanding is happening in our spiritual questing. We are moving beyond the view that 'God's Will' is a fixed statement somewhere in the sky, with which we have to comply, towards an understanding of life as an ongoing, dynamic *process* through which God is weaving his Dream. To engage with this process we must move beyond the car park picnic, and risk the climb into the unknown. It is no longer a question of 'my salvation' or the pursuit of a particular religious tradition, but of the evolution of all creation towards its interrelated wholeness. We can only participate in this process if we are willing to move forward in trusting, and trustworthy, companionship with each other and with the Lord who climbs ahead of us, seeking out the right anchor points for our personal and our communal journeying.

Spend a little time, in your imagination, with these two ways of finding 'security' in the mountainous landscape of life: the solid ground from which to view the scenery, or the rope and the companions whom you can trust.

- Which approach has been your chosen option so far?
- In which of these places do you feel you are now?
- Which will you choose from now on, as the basis for your Kingdom journey?

As a model for this kind of interrelatedness, God himself speaks of being 'in us and we in him' and we express our very limited understanding of the mystery of God as 'three persons in One'. The idea of 'trinity', far from being a mind-boggling theological peculiarity, turns out to be a gentle, but inescapable reminder that in the core of our being we are all held in a web of interrelatedness, in which each of us affects all of us, and each part is co-responsible for the whole. In the end, the only truth we can trust is this assurance that we are each held in this wholeness, and that the wholeness, who is God, is to be trusted, just as the climbers trust the rope.

Easy to talk of trusting something as vague as 'truth'! What does it really mean? And how do we begin to do it?

You might like to reflect on three ways that I have personally found helpful:

- Getting in touch with the truth within us, which guides us, like a compass in our hearts, and shows us when we are 'living true' and when we are being false to ourselves and to others.
- Noticing examples in the world around us of what it might mean to 'live true' and to make a positive difference to human life.

- Learning from Jesus himself the meaning of the True Life, and responding to this model by making our own choices and decisions according to these values.

The Truth within us

The effects of sin, as we have seen, are cumulative. From delusion and deception down to the darkest recesses of violence and destruction. But if sin is cumulative, so surely, is grace! The entanglements of sin, both personal and structural, drag us down the deadly spiral. But every step we take with the Lord along the Kingdom path draws us a little closer to the true life that he embodies – the true life that in the core of our being we so long to live ourselves.

When we commit ourselves to the Kingdom Venture we are making a radical turnaround. The underlying direction of our lives becomes aligned with the direction and purpose of Life itself. There will be many times when we will slip back into the former destructive alignments, but if we take the time and space to be close to God in prayer, we will soon learn to *know* when we are 'running true' and when we are 'off course'. This process of becoming familiar with the stirrings in our own hearts is often called 'discernment'. We sift our experience, and learn to notice, with increasing sensitivity, when we are being drawn by the promptings of the Holy Spirit, and all that is creative in us, and when we are being driven by the destructive movements that we looked at in Chapter 2. In his poem 'The Wreck of the Deutschland', Gerard Manley Hopkins speaks of 'soft sift in an hourglass', and this is also a beautiful image of the process of discernment.

We could also say that discernment is like a compass in the core of our own being. In turning to God and choosing to commit ourselves to the growth of God's Kingdom, we have aligned our course with the True North of God's own Dream for creation. When we deflect from all that is most true within us, this inner compass will wobble and waver, and we will know that we need to take corrective action. The process of discernment is explored more fully in the companion book *Landmarks*.

One way to 'tune in' to this inner compass is to reflect, regularly, over how we are feeling and reacting to the various events and encounters in our lives. A helpful way of doing this is to use what is commonly called the 'Review of Consciousness' prayer, or the 'Examen', or 'Review of the Day'.

Reviewing the day with God

Perhaps your days seem to rush by, leaving no time for prayer. Or perhaps they stretch out like an eternity? Perhaps you feel that God hasn't had any part in the day's events. We very easily lose all sight of God's presence as we live our daily lives, but he never loses sight of us. Take a few minutes at the end of the day just to reflect on what has been happening, and reconnect your daily life with your life in God. Try to make this kind of prayer part of your daily routine.

Begin by asking God to show you how he has been present and active in the events of the day, and to shed his light on your own memories and feelings about what has been happening.

Let the day's events replay, like a video in fast forward, and just notice anything that particularly catches your attention. Stay with that memory, as if you were 'pausing' the video to look more closely at that part.

Look back over anything you feel grateful for. Just relive it in your memory. Express your thanks to God for it in your own words, or without words. Maybe there was a meeting with someone, or a letter, or a friendly gesture? Did something make you laugh, or move you to tears? Has a problem been solved, or did you notice something in God's creation that made you feel joy?

Remember those who deserve your gratitude for the blessings the day has brought. Those who provided the food you ate, or the essential services. Those who did something for you that they didn't need to do. Remember something in the day that you yourself can be proud of. (We often find this difficult.)

Just reflect over these things quietly. What has drawn you closer to God today? What have you learned about God and his Kingdom today? What happened to make you feel loved? Were you able to give a sign of love to another person?

Was there any time or situation during the day when you feel that your 'inner compass' was running true? Remember that experience and store it as a reference point for your onward journey.

Was there any situation in which you feel you were being untrue to yourself? Does this experience make you want to change anything in your course for the way ahead?

Are there any dark patches during the day? Is there something that you now wish you had handled differently? Is there some hurt that you are still carrying, caused by someone else? If so, simply express your feelings to God, as a child might talk to a loving parent. You may feel that the day has been unspeakably awful, and it's OK to tell God about those feelings.

Maybe something has left you feeling inadequate or fearful or resentful? Be still with these feelings for a while, and notice, if you can, where they may have their roots. Like the brambles in our unmade garden, the roots of unease in our living are often a long way from the place where these feelings show themselves in the outer surface of our lives. You might feel drawn to ask God to show you the deeper reasons for any nega-tive feelings or reactions during the day, and for guidance on how you might open these roots up to his healing and enlightenment.

End your prayer by asking for God's continuing blessing upon tomorrow's living, as you let yourself sink into his loving care for you.

Echoes of the Kingdom: the True Life in Real Life

The world, as I experience it in my daily life, is not as 'secular' as the Church would sometimes have us believe. On the contrary, the world is profoundly spiritual. It is God's own self-expression (albeit grievously marred by the human desire for autonomy) and it is, as Gerard Manley Hopkins says, 'charged with the grandeur of God'.

When I reflect on the call to be a partner with Jesus in the venture of redemption, I find it helpful to look around me and notice what I find in my own lived experience, that *enthuses* me with Kingdom values. Where do I see them in action? What helps me out of the despondency of sin into an active desire to be a Kingdom-builder?

An inspiring way to do this is to reflect on those places or people or events where we hear 'echoes of the Kingdom'. It isn't easy, initially, to imagine ourselves alongside Jesus, being called into active discipleship. We may find it easier to begin by picking up some of these 'echoes'.

I only need to look back over the past week to find several incidents that have made me feel 'alive' in this kind of way. These events have been living demonstrations of the Kingdom journey, each in its own way, though in most cases the people concerned would never have used this kind of language about themselves.

One morning, for example, I was travelling north from London on an early train. I found myself sitting beside two young people, perhaps in their early twenties, a man and a woman, both smartly dressed, obviously re-presenting their employer. It was impossible not to hear their conversation as we travelled north. They were architects, on their way to a meeting to plan an urban renewal project for a derelict area on Merseyside. They were eagerly discussing their ideas and poring over aerial photos of the site. What gripped me most of all was that their entire conversation revolved not around how much money could be made from such a venture, but on how they personally could best address the real needs of the people concerned. In everything they said, they were focused on the people who would be affected by their decisions. How might they keep a distance between the 'workplaces' and the residential areas of their new township? How could they ensure the safety and well-being of children playing in its streets? How could they squeeze in more parkland and open green space? How easy would it be for people to reach recreational facilities? What kind of landscape would greet people as they looked out of their kitchen windows? How could they reclaim yet more land from the scourge of dereliction and pollution? In short, the energy and intellect of these two young people was being lovingly applied to what, in Christian terms, we would call 'renewing the face of the earth'. When I reached my destination I wanted to hug them both and thank them for their loving care of a planet and its people. Instead, I smiled my greetings and left them quietly to get on with their Kingdom work, never knowing whether or not they knew the King for whom they were working.

During the course of the week I watched three documentary programmes on television. One showed boatloads of Japanese tourists visiting Pearl Harbour, where their ancestors had rained destruction during the Second World War. I watched them fall into a deep and solemn silence. I watched the tears travelling across their faces, and touched into their deep and genuine sadness, that such a peaceful harbour should be the sanctuary of such terrible memories. They had taken a lot of trouble, and spent a lot of money, to make this pilgrimage. It was a penitential journey that each of us has reason to make in our own way, to some part of the earth in whose destruction we have colluded. It was a Kingdom journey.

The second programme was about dolphin therapy. It told the story of a doctor in the United States who spends enormous amounts of time and patience coaxing autistic children into some kind of communication. He has discovered that such children relate more readily to dolphins than to human beings, so he works with the dolphins as his allies in this project of bringing life where there is none. It may take weeks, months, years, before a child speaks a first long-awaited word or reveals a gesture of recognition. But this doctor waits. Doctor, child and dolphin – a trinity of love, and hope, and patience.

The third programme included a report from the Isle of Man. All the island's primary school children had been given an acorn to grow. The time had come for the resulting seedlings to be planted out. I watched four thousand children converge, with their teachers, to plant a forest to celebrate the turn of the millennium. And I remembered that God grows an eternal Kingdom from our tiny seeds of faith. If I needed proof that this was an act of redemption, I only needed to look into the shining, eager eyes of the children, and the steady, encouraging expression of their teachers. Generations yet unborn will walk through the pathways of the forest we sow with our lives' seeds.

Truly, the Kingdom is all around us, and the Reign of God is already redeeming the face of the earth. All we need are eyes to see and ears to hear.

Echoes of the Kingdom continue to reverberate through every day and every moment. We hear, for example, about increasing numbers of young professional men and women leaving their 'upwardly mobile' lifestyle to offer voluntary service at home and overseas. We notice how teenagers look out for one another in the streets and nightclubs of our dangerous cities, and we see the amazing generosity to appeals like Children in Need. These are echoes of God's creating Word and responses to the same deep calling – the call of the King.

During the course of the coming week, take notice of anything you see on television, or read in the papers, or experience directly in your daily life, that fires your enthusiasm to respond to God's call to become a Kingdom-builder. Look out for your own 'Yes! events'.

Listen to the voice of Christ calling to you through those stories. How do you want to respond to what you see and hear?

For some people, the most effective inspiration to become part of the Kingdom Venture is that of an individual who is living a visibly God-centred life. Perhaps you have your own favourite 'saint'. Is there anyone who has crossed your path – either remotely or intimately – someone who has embodied for you something of what it means to be a Kingdom-builder? What is it, in particular, that you admire and feel drawn to emulate in that person's life?

If you could tell your children one story of a human life that made, or is making, a difference, whose story would you tell?

Entering into the True Life

The only way to share Christ's work and mission is actually to enter into his life. We have seen that we have access to an 'inner compass' that indicates 'true north' in the core of our being when we are really 'living true', but wobbles and shakes when we are being untrue to ourselves. And we have noticed that there are countless examples of other human stories that reflect the True Life in their own ways for us.

But a compass needs a point of reference, and this brings us to the heart of God's call. He gives us an absolute point of reference in the life, death and resurrection of Jesus. Jesus is an embodiment of the True Life that is God's Dream for all. We can learn to trust that Truth by allowing our own lives to be increasingly conformed to Jesus' life. One obvious and very practical way of doing this is to ask, in any situation of choice or doubt: 'What would Jesus have done?' Sometimes the answers to this question will seriously challenge the way we do things, and the way 'the church' does things. Are we ready for this kind of challenge?

And how do we know what Jesus would have done? This question brings us to the whole point of the Kingdom journey. We discover what Jesus would have done by going with him along the way and learning from him, in all the situations that he faced during his lived ministry. A powerful way of doing this is to enter into the Gospel scenes in your imagination, and become, yourself, a participant in them. If you are unfamiliar with this approach to prayer, try the following exercise, using any Gospel scene you choose.

Entering into the Gospel in imaginative prayer

Your imagination can be the place where two worlds meet: the world of Gospel truth and the world of your daily life. Here are some suggestions for joining Jesus in the Gospel stories and becoming a part of what you see and read.

Choose a Gospel story that especially appeals to you (one of the healing miracles, for example). Ask God to be your Guide as you enter into the story. Read the passage through slowly, maybe several times if you wish, and then relax and let yourself imagine the scene.

What can you see, hear, smell, taste or feel? What is the weather like? What seems to be happening in the scene? Now begin to populate your scene. Is anyone else there? Anyone you recognise? What kind of 'atmosphere' does the scene suggest?

Does any part of the scene attract you particularly, or bring up strong feelings in you? If so, focus especially on that part and explore it more deeply.

Now let the action of the scene unfold and take your own place in it. Where do you find yourself in the scene? Perhaps you are one of the crowd, or one of the disciples. Perhaps you feel like an outsider looking in, or you may identify with the person being healed, or challenged, or invited into a new relationship with the Lord. Don't make any judgements, or force yourself to be where you think you *ought* to be. The power of this prayer is to recognise the place where you really feel you are, and to let the light of Christ shine upon that place.

How are you feeling about what is happening in your scene? Disturbed? Attracted? Curious? Afraid? Eager? Just notice and acknowledge your feelings. Don't try to censor them.

Do you feel drawn to speak with anyone there? What do you want to say? Do you feel that anything is being said to you? Can you enter into a conversation with Jesus?

If you have noticed at any point that one part of the scene has brought up especially strong feelings in you (either positive or negative), go back in your imagination to that particular part. Don't force anything, but just ask God to lead you into what is specially important for you in that part. The feelings you have are coming from deep down, and they have something to tell you. Ask God to help you explore them.

End your time of prayer by thanking God for his presence with you and for anything he has shown you. Maybe end with a familiar prayer.

As we set out to walk alongside Jesus through his living and his dying, this method of prayer will be our key to discovering more and more about his Truth, and conforming our lives to that Truth.

In Chapter 2 we faced the awesome possibility that our own personal cell within the Body of Christ is diseased and dysfunctional, and may even be cancerous, with the potential to be life-threatening to others. The call to the Kingdom Venture is not just a call to become a healthy cell again, for our own sake or for the sake of personal eternal life. It is a call to allow our personal, healed cell to be reintegrated into the whole Body, and reconnected to the Web of Being. Once reintegrated into the Body, that cell is called into action, to fulfil its own personal role within the Body. It is a call to mission, and to the building of God's Kingdom.

We are called:

- To be healed, so that we might become healers.
- To be forgiven, so that we might be bearers of mercy.
- To be taught, so that we might become teachers.
- To be calmed, so that we might become peace-makers.
- To be challenged in our untruths, so that we might become challengers of untruth.
- To be restored to life, so that we might become life-givers.
- To eat with Jesus, so that we might learn to share our bread.
- To be homeless with Jesus, so that we might discover the joy of pilgrimage.
- To experience the destitution of 'nothing to lose', so that we might discover we have everything to hope for.

A prayer of commitment

The King calls you to enlist in the Kingdom Venture. If your heart says 'Yes' to such a call – or even if all you can summon is the *desire* to be able to say 'Yes' – then you might like to express your response in your own words, along these lines:

Creator God, source of all creation
I come into an awareness of your presence
Knowing myself to be just a small and broken,
yet loved and cherished piece of that creation.
And knowing that in this timeless moment I am in the presence
Of all those you call your own, past, present and to come.

That which is of you, deep in the core of my being
Makes me long to be part of the great adventure
Of making your Dream for creation a reality on this planet Earth.
It makes me long to be alongside you,
Living out my part of your Christ-life in this world.

I know that this may lead me into sorrow, as well as joy.
The road may bring rejection and misunderstanding
and even pain and poverty, both material and spiritual.
Yet, deep down, this is what I really desire:
To be with you in this venture.

This is what I choose, as the guiding principle of my life,
In whatever way reflects your Dream for me.
Let my dream and your Dream become one.
This is my response to the call of your Life
Vibrating deep in my own heart.
Please draw me ever more deeply into your Way.

4. A DECISIVE INTERVENTION

If you have come this far on the journey you will have made an inner commitment, in your own time and your own way, to make whatever change of direction is required to align your own dreams with the Dream God is dreaming with you and within you. It will be part of your deepest desiring to attune your life's choices and decisions to the inner compass within you that continually indicates the direction of the heart of God.

You are looking for relationship with God, and God is longing for the full restoration of relationship with you. He longs for it so much that he is prepared to intervene decisively into the human story. He is ready, quite literally, to fall in love with you.

Falling into love

In a remarkable film, *The City of Angels*, the story is told of an angel, who calls himself Seth. In the film, Seth and his like are seen to be present to the human community of Los Angeles in a number of ways. They are especially present on the boundaries of life and death, giving unseen encouragement, healing unacknowledged hurts, accompanying the dying across the threshold to a new dimension of life. To almost all human eyes they are invisible, with the occasional exception of those on the brink of death, or of small children. The film director shows them as human beings of normal appearance, except for a deep calm on their faces, which marks them out as being grounded 'somewhere else'. However, they have no sense perceptions, no ability to feel, physically, either the tenderness or the pain of human living.

Seth, however, falls in love with a doctor in the hospital where he has been attending the dying. Gradually, over time, this doctor becomes aware of Seth's presence, and is able to see him and talk with him. Her reaction is a strange mingling of fear and love. Fear of the unknown. Love for the depth of the unseen mystery which Seth represents.

In due course, Seth learns from another angel that it is possible to become human, if one really so desires. Seth desires this more than anything. He desires to become a fully embodied human being, who can feel everything that his beloved feels and experience human life as she does. He longs to *express* his love for her in a way that she will understand and respond to.

But the cost of such a choice is high. In fact it is higher than Seth can guess or imagine. As an angel he is not subject to the laws of time and space. He can be wherever he wishes to be, whenever he wishes it. He feels emotion in his heart, but nothing with his senses, and is therefore immune to physical pain. He is eternal. He is invulnerable. And he is in constant communion with God.

At the crucial moment of decision we find Seth sitting on a crane, high – immeasurably high, it seems – above the city. He looks down upon all of human life, teeming beneath him. It was at this point in the film that I was taken, in my imagination, to the crucial moment when God, Father, Son and Holy Spirit, looked down upon creation. Perhaps we can imagine God seeing something like the scene Seth saw, as his eternal eye zoomed in on our world:

- A seething surge of light and darkness, with the city traffic weaving its way along highways and byways.
- Streets jammed with people, busy about their urgent concerns, or slumped in dark corners, waiting for the drop of small change into the waiting hat.
- People dying, in the street, at home and in hospitals. Children coming to birth in maternity ward, or ghetto.
- The able-bodied, on their way to the gym, and the crippled, inching their way through the maelstrom of life, every step accompanied by pain.
- Street fights and lone gunmen, and parents patching up children's squabbles.
- Addicts, pushers and rehab workers, the captives and the free.
- Rape and murder, stalking lonely alleys, and night nurses, watching late over beds of pain.
- Springtime bursting out in leaf and blossom, and fields devastated by plague and pollution.
- Homes aglow with evening light behind closed curtains, and homes where children dread the footstep at the bedroom door.

- Newly-weds celebrating the first joy of love, and the disillusioned in the divorce courts.
- Children in school, and children in distress.
- Inflicters of hurting, victims of hurting, healers of hurting.

… God's eye view of God's creation.

Spend a little time with God as he looks down upon *your* world and upon your own neighbourhood. What do *you* see? How do you feel? What might you want to say to God about what you see and feel?

In the film, Seth takes the decision to let himself fall. This is the only way in which he can be one with his beloved, and engage fully in her human life. In a dramatic sequence, we see him throw himself off the crane and we watch as he plummets down to earth. At first the journey has the quality of what, so we might imagine, a birth canal might be like – the sudden and unpredictable plunge into a way of being which is wholly unknown, yet full of potential. Then Seth lands on the hard ground.

- His invulnerability has been surrendered, and his body takes the brunt of the fall. As he lies on the ground, in a pool of his own blood, he has his first experience of physical anguish, and of mockery and scorn, as nearby building workers make fun of him.
- His heavenly mobility has been surrendered. As he tries to get on a bus to travel to his beloved, he realises that he has no money. He faces the blank, rejecting wall that the world presents to the poor and the penniless.
- His innocence and trust have been surrendered. When he tries to take a cab, he is mugged and left for dead in a city underpass.
- The deep simplicity of eternal life, and the unbroken communion with God and with his fellow angels has turned into the complexity and tension of minute-by-minute survival in a potentially very hostile en-vironment. Falling in love has sentenced Seth to rejection, struggle, suffering and death. Will love be worth it?

Just a Hollywood movie, of course … But for me this story brought to life the reality of God's intervention into human life in a new and vivid way. For the first time I was able to see, in graphic realism, something of the cost of God's falling in love with me, with you, with all of God's creation.

As Christians we believe that 'God sent his only Son into the world, so that the world through him might be saved'. At this point in our journey, we pause to reflect on the cost of that 'sending', and its effects. Seth's story helps us to do this reflecting in a way that mirrors the reality of our twenty-first-century world. It refuses to spare us the truth about what was surrendered so that Jesus might be born among us, and what depth of love and longing inspired such a surrender of Jesus' eternal life with the Father. We might think, especially, of what it meant for God himself freely to choose to be:

- constrained to be in just one place, one family, one culture, one short period of time, even while he was longing to touch the heart of all creation everywhere and throughout all time;
- exposed to the possibility of every kind of human pain and human feeling;
- fragmented by the conflicting demands and pressures of living in the space-time continuum;
- without material cushioning in a world that pushes the small and the weak to the wall.

Was our love worth the cost? Perhaps only God could answer that question.

Seth had to set out to search for the beloved, for whom he had surrendered heaven and accepted the brutal realities and crippling limitations of life on earth. She wasn't standing waiting for him to arrive. Jesus has the same problem. We, for whom he came down to earth, at such a cost, are not standing waiting to receive him. The search goes on for us. Sometimes it takes a lifetime to find us. Sometimes, it might seem, the search is in vain. Yet still he searches. He lives out that search now in *our* lives, and every time there is a response from one for whom his heart yearns, he invites that person to join in the ongoing search, until all are found and touched by the love of God.

Weaving a space for God

In Chapter 2 we noticed the tiny detail given to us by the Genesis author, that after the Fall of Adam and Eve, God continued to show his care for them by making tunics for them out of animal skins. Even in the depths

of his disappointment, God picks up the pieces of his Dream, and continues to weave, and re-weave, the lost wholeness and communion of
Creator and Creation. Nothing – not even the worst that human beings
can think or do – can prevent or subvert the process of God's ongoing
creative energy and love.

Now the time has come to experience the sequel to that weaving. We
might imagine God's gaze deepening in on a particular home in a particular town or village of this troubled earth, focusing on one year, one day,
one hour, out of all time, seeking out one receptive individual, and asking
the question: *'Since life began, I have clothed creation in its physical form. I have
breathed my spirit into human bodies and given you the earth to till, so that life
might be sustained. Now I ask you: will you weave a body of humanness for me?
I need a tunic of humanness in which I can become one with my creation. Will you
make that human body for my eternal presence? Will you give birth to my love, in
your own life, so that all creation might be restored to wholeness?'*

God's intervention into human history hangs upon this moment. A
moment in time – in the little known and ill-regarded town of Nazareth –
but also a moment *out of time*, when God asks for space to become
incarnate in God's own creation. We know, and acknowledge, that the
redemption story hangs upon the consent of a young girl in Nazareth,
Mary, engaged to be married to a local carpenter called Joseph. We can
imagine heaven and earth holding their breath as the angel awaits Mary's
reply. But we can also distance ourselves from the whole encounter, put
Mary into a glass case and surround her with flowers, and avoid the
personal consequences of this moment. Because God asks not just Mary
of Nazareth, but each and every one of us, to make him a human home,
in our own bodies, minds, hearts and lives, where his redeeming work
may be continued. He asks for the broken threads of our own, personal
human experience, and promises to weave them into his Dream for all
creation.

The question is put to us over and over again as we live our lives.
Sometimes we will say 'Yes', with wholehearted assent. Sometimes the
fears will win out, and we will hold back. Every time we say 'Yes', we
affirm our own deepest longings for wholeness and communion. Every
time we say 'No', we frustrate what we most long for.

Read and reflect on the story of the Annunciation, in Luke 1:26-38. The angel has a message for you. Listen to that message. What is God saying to your heart through these words? How do you feel? Don't censor your feelings. Whatever they are, whether apparently negative or positive, or a confused mixture of the two, let them be there in your prayer, and lay them before God just as they are. He will weave himself a human home out of the material of your life in whatever ways you allow, but he will never use force to persuade you.

The 'blank cheque' of 'Let your Dream be dreamed in me', which is being asked of us, is the first consequence of our commitment to the Way of the Kingdom. It may well stir questions in us. How can I make over my life to a process that is pure mystery? What will happen next if I give God permission to make his home in me? Will he ask more of me than I can give?

The journey we are now beginning *is* a mystery. We are asked to get on board the train with no knowledge of its destination. *This* is faith. And faith is *trust*. Our Christian faith, we discover, is not just a matter of assenting to creed and doctrine, nor even of any amount of faithful observation or religious duty. What is being asked of us is our willing and wholehearted participation in a living, dynamic process. God asks us to become living cells in the Body of Christ. If we say 'Yes', the life, and the death, and the resurrection of Jesus of Nazareth will become incarnate in *us*, and will be *continued* in us. It begins with the germination of God's seed within our hearts – the Godseed on which we reflected in Chapter 1. It leads, in ways only known to God, to the coming of God's reign on earth. It is the start, for each searching heart, of the Kingdom Venture.

Pregnant with God

God has fallen in love with us – quite literally, God has come down to earth, and opened Godself to all the raw brutality, as well as the warm tenderness, of human life. The result of that falling into love is that God has made earth pregnant with Godself. But not in some mystical, ethereal way. No! God's human life is within us, literally made flesh in our own bodies, minds and lives. We ourselves are made of the same elements that were present in the Big Bang. We are made of stardust. We are quite literally the children of the universe. And God's request of us is that we allow God to become incorporated in every way into our earthed reality.

From the moment of our 'Yes' (and our 'Yes' is called forth again and again, in everything we do and choose) we are pregnant with the redeeming presence of God's own self, whom we call his Son. In our personal living and dying we will live out our own unique fragment of the redemption story, but we can no more predict how this will be than a pregnant mother can predict the future course of her baby's life.

To choose to bring a child into this world is an act of faith. To choose to bring God into this world is a commitment to a life of faith, worked out moment by moment in all our days.

Mary appears to have been overwhelmed by the angel's presence, and so enfolded in God's love that 'No' was not an option. Perhaps there have been moments in your life like that, when the palpable presence and power of God caused you to gasp and say: 'Whatever it costs, I want to be a part of this venture.' Then the everyday reality kicks in once more, and you wonder – as surely Mary must have done – what you have let yourself in for. We might travel with her, as she tries to deal with the consequences of her choice: with Joseph's reaction, and that of her parents; with the attitude of the neighbours, and of the religious authorities. In their eyes, after all, her inexplicable pregnancy was reason enough to put her to death by stoning.

Reflect on the cost of your own 'Yes'. Have you had to face hostility, or scorn, or misunderstanding, from those close to you, because you are choosing to allow God to become incarnate in your life? How do you feel about it? Bring your feelings to God in your prayer. God is the Father of the Christ-life you are carrying. He is longing for what he has fathered in you to come to fullness and he will move heaven and earth to hold you safe and sure throughout your 'pregnancy'.

Reflect on any experience in your own life of natural or adoptive parenting, or of the care of children you love. What you feel for them is only a shadow of what God the Father feels for you, as you bring his Son to birth.

Mary did what any of us might have done in the circumstances. She sought out solitude, to think over all that was happening to her. She looked for a safe place where she would be welcomed and received, where she would be listened to as she told her amazing story. She went to find a friend who would be alongside her, as she processed the events that had placed her in this supremely blessed, and supremely vulnerable position. Mary set out to a nearby hill town, to visit her cousin Elizabeth, who was also six months' pregnant, even though everyone had thought she was far too old to bear children. The very young Mary sought out the older, wiser Elizabeth. Their time together has a message for us, as we seek to come to terms with what it means to be 'pregnant with God'.

Read and reflect on the story of Mary's visit to Elizabeth, in Luke 1:39-56. Do you have an 'Elizabeth' in your life – a friend, a 'soul-friend', whom you trust completely to understand who you really are and to listen to your story and see the deeper meanings in it? If so, you might like to spend a little time with that person, at this point in the Kingdom journey. Tell them what you are doing, and how you are feeling about it. Share with them that moment when you first felt the touch of God's love in your life, and the unique way in which God came upon you, overshadowed you, and asked you to let your life be a home in which his Son might come to birth.

When Elizabeth sees her cousin Mary, pregnant with Jesus, her own unborn child, who will become John the Baptist, moves in her womb, as if to greet the unborn child in Mary. In my experience this is a reflection of what happens when two 'soul friends' meet. When we greet each other as fellow Kingdom travellers, the still unborn Christ growing in each of us gives a little leap of joy in recognition of the still unborn Christ growing in the other. You might like to notice, and share this moment of recognition with your 'Elizabeth', and celebrate it in some special way that is meaningful to you both.

Not a crown, but a footprint

In her beautiful book of Celtic reflections (*The Celtic Spirit*), Caitlín Matthews reminds us of how different were the inauguration ceremonies of the early Gaelic rulers from today's elaborate coronations. The Celtic kings occupied not a throne, but a *stone* – a sacred stone, which was the symbol of their kingship. One of these, in western Scotland, has the impression of a footprint in it, on which the new ruler would stand, in the footsteps of his ancestors.

In Chapter 3 we made our own response to the call of the King to engage in his Kingdom Venture. It need not surprise us that this King is not to be found in the usual places, or surrounded by regal pomp and posturing. He is a king of footprints, not of throne and crown. He establishes his Kingdom by walking the earth.

Jesus of Nazareth walked one small part of this earth in one neglected outpost of the Roman Empire, two thousand years ago. He made contact with a few thousand people, at most, and touched just a few aspects of the brokenness of creation with his human hands. I used to find it frustrating (and indeed I have often told God about my frustrations!) that this Jesus never knew, for example, how it feels to be a woman, or a mother, or a wife. He never lived out the life of a parent trying to protect his child from the drugs scene. He never tackled the pressures of modern education, or the stress of an exploitative work-place. He never knew the agony of an unwanted pregnancy, or the slow deterioration of senility. The list of things that Jesus never knew or experienced in his earthly life is endless.

But my frustration turned to a new sense of wonder when I began to realise that this is precisely why Jesus called us his friends, his brothers and sisters, the Body of Christ, and his beloved family. Together we are called to live out every possible aspect of what it means to be human, and to do so with him, in him and through him, so that through our infinite variety of living, and dying, every possible pathway of humanity can be touched by his redeeming love. We are, as Teresa of Avila puts it, the hands and feet, the eyes and ears and hearts of Jesus now. He lives in our brokenness because that is exactly what he came to make whole. He commissions us to live out the redemption story in our own story.

This makes me see my own problems and weaknesses very differently. No longer are they the places I want to hide from him until I have straightened them out. No! They are the most important places of all, because that is where he is doing one part of his redeeming work for all creation. The things I most dislike about myself, and my relationships with the people who cause me the worst pain are the cutting edge of the redemption process.

So if we are to be incorporated into God's work of salvation, if we are to be active cells in the Body of Christ, we too must walk! We must place our feet in the footprints of Jesus. He calls us to follow where he leads. But he also calls us to lead so that others may follow. The mission into which we are called is a journey – a continuous process through which God is redeeming all creation and renewing the face of the earth.

The road to Bethlehem

The walk begins in Nazareth. We too, once the Christ-life has germinated in our hearts, find ourselves, like Mary and Joseph, required to walk. Some of this walking is physical, involving real journeys to real places, with real people. Some of it is an inner walk, to new attitudes and new levels of understanding and trust. Let us accompany them now through the months following the Annunciation, and discover what we may have to learn from this journey, as we try to place our own feet in the footprints of the Lord.

Perhaps the most obvious thing about this journey is that it encounters a whole series of setbacks. I find this enormously encouraging, at one level, since setbacks are something I can relate to!

The first setback is Joseph's very understandable reaction to Mary's announcement that she is pregnant. Even in our own 'enlightened' times, such a disclosure would be quite enough to bring most engagements to a stormy conclusion, if not worse. The child is not his, so much is clear. Is he really to believe Mary's story that she was 'overwhelmed by the Holy Spirit'?

Take time to imagine yourself in Mary's situation. Then do the same for Joseph. Become present to the deadlock between them. Does their breakdown in communication ring any bells in your own experience? Feel the helplessness in each of them, to resolve this intractable problem that threatens their love. Then sink, in your prayer, into Joseph's dream (Matthew 1:18-25). Listen again to the angel's words to Mary: 'Nothing is impossible to God' (Luke 1:37).

The second setback comes from beyond the immediate family. Mary and Joseph are compelled to go to Bethlehem to comply with the census requirements. This is the last thing they need, in the late stages of Mary's pregnancy, and their frustration, and even anger, can well be imagined. It feels like a man-made complication that might jeopardise the safe birth of the child.

In fact it becomes the first of many examples in the New Testament of the way God weaves his Meaning out of our confusion and brings what is creative out of what has all the potential to be destructive. It is, perhaps, a much needed antidote to the emotional shock the couple has come through, to journey together, dependent on each other, caring for each other and for the coming child in hostile conditions. It is an opportunity

The burden we carry may be an unborn Christ

to strengthen the bond between them, and maybe to talk to each other in new ways about all that the future holds. Most importantly, it is a summons back to their roots.

Many people who pray this passage imaginatively discover a fondness for the donkey. Let yourself be aware of the donkey, as you travel this road in prayer. Let him remind you that although the road you walk often seems lonely and hard, you are being carried. We carry each other in the community of faith, and God carries us all.

Are there any 'man-made complications' in your own life – things you could so well do without? Perhaps you feel that circumstances place obstacles in your path of following the Lord? If so, let them be set out in your prayer, without any judgement of yourself or of others, and ask God to enlighten the darkness that clusters round them.

If you feel drawn to do so, come alongside Mary and Joseph on the road to Bethlehem. Tell them about your own life's 'journey' and your own feelings about 'bringing the Lord to birth' in your life. Listen as they tell you their story. Let yourself be present to the new life, growing visibly now in Mary's womb. How do you feel about the nearness of the unborn Lord? Is there anything you would like to say to him? What you say to the unborn Lord in Mary, you are also saying to the unborn Lord in your own life's womb. Listen to anything you feel he may be saying to you.

Don't forget the donkey. Who carries *you* when you are weary or in despair, or when the road is simply too long? Let that person come into your prayer, and express your thanks to God for them in your own way. Are there people who rely on *you* to carry *them*? Talk to the donkey about your weariness and listen to him as he shares his story with you. Often the burden we carry is the Christ in disguise. How do you feel about this?

The next setback is encountered when the little party reaches Bethlehem. The town is packed out. Every room is booked and the streets are milling with the thousands of others who have made the journey back to their ancestral home, in order to comply with the registration requirements.

Remember how the unborn John the Baptist leapt in Elizabeth's womb at the approach of the unborn Christ in Mary's? Now the opposite situation arises. Imagine Joseph knocking on one door after another, as Mary waits in the shadows, her back aching, her heart full of anxiety. 'No room here any more!' 'Sorry, we're overflowing.' 'A room for two – you've got to be joking!' And maybe some of the innkeepers noticed the bulge of Mary's advanced pregnancy, and shied away from the possible consequences of giving this couple accommodation.

Over and over, all through the streets of Bethlehem, the unborn Christ is greeted with the words and the spirit of rejection and exclusion. The Calvary journey begins here in Bethlehem, where the Christ-Child experiences, for the first of many times, what it means to be 'despised and rejected'. And Mary and Joseph experience it too! If we would be the bearers and carriers of Christ, this is a sign of what we must expect to experience.

Eventually there is the slightest softening of heart. We could compare it to a single star, shining out in a black sky – flickering unsteadily, perhaps, but nevertheless a source of light and hope. One innkeeper feels compassion for the weary couple at his door. He offers them makeshift accommodation down in the stable, with the animals. 'At least it's a shelter,' he ventures to suggest, 'and no one will disturb you down there.'

Read and reflect on the story of Jesus' birth in Luke 2:1-7. Try to imagine yourself alongside Mary and Joseph as they look for a place to spend the night. Notice your own feelings. Where do you find yourself in the story? Does any particular moment in the story leap to life for you, perhaps because something reminds you of memories and feelings from your own experience? If so, stay with that moment and try to deepen into it, asking God to show you what he is revealing to you through it.

Be in Bethlehem in your prayer through the long hours of that Holy Night. Watch the events of the night unfold. How do you feel about the presence of this tiny new life that is coming to birth in the 'stable' of your own experience. There was no chance to sweep the cellars clean. God has chosen – freely chosen – to express his over-whelming love for you by coming 'down to earth' to dwell in the stable of *your* life. He doesn't mind how cramped and inadequate the space you make over to him. The tiniest sliver of your heart is enough for him to take root and grow. Is this what you desire? What might you want to say to him, if anything? What do you feel you want to do?

Gifting

The birth of a baby almost always attracts visitors, who frequently come bearing gifts. As events unfold in Bethlehem, out on the nearby hills the shepherds are keeping the night watch with their flocks. Shepherds were very much at the lower end of the social scale of the times. From the very beginning, it seems, God has chosen to reveal himself to the most unlikely among us first, and commission those he chooses to carry the message out into the wider world. The last people to hear of the coming of God appear to be the ones who expected to be first.

It would seem, also, that God chooses to reveal himself to the quiet and the watchful, because, as we hear, some 'wise men from the East' – perhaps philosophers, or astronomers, or simply people who had cultivated the habit of keeping their eyes and minds open to events in the universe around them – were on their way to the Child.

One thing that both these events give us is an insight into how to respond to the Christ-life which is coming to birth in each other – including those who are not visibly 'Christian' and not members of any 'church'. Let us beware of assuming that God only comes to birth in the places and the people where we expect to find him. The story of the shepherds and the magi show us that this is far from the case. When I stop to reflect on what their actions show me, I see a guiding pattern for how I might respond myself to the Christ-life coming to birth in those around me:

- First the visitors 'go to see this thing which is come to pass'. They go to where the Christ is being born. For us, this might be a call to go out into the world and simply allow ourselves to become aware of the very many ways in which God is coming to birth in the events and the people of our planet, whether or not we – or they – happen to think they are 'religious'.
- When they discover the Christ-life – in the least expected place and circumstances – they *revere* what they find. Let us do so too. When we discover evidence of the Christ-life in our fellow human beings – however unexpectedly – *let us revere what we find*. And let us do so authentically, sincerely, and with no hidden agenda of hooking them into our own way of worship.
- Only then, having discovered and revered the Christ, do they offer whatever gifting they can bring. We, who call ourselves Christians, have much to give from the treasure that has been given to us, but let us offer it humbly and sensitively, and always in the awareness that the Christ coming to birth in the other person will have as much to give as we have to offer. Whenever the Christ in one of us meets the Christ in another, there will be an *exchange* of gifts. Let this thought protect us from the patronising attitude that we must 'convert' the other to our own way of living the Christ-life.
- Finally, the visitors return to where they came from – transformed by the experience, and ready to leave the continuing story to God.

Read and ponder the story of the visit of the magi, in Matthew 2:1-12. Where have you found the Christ coming to birth in unexpected circumstances? How did you react? Who has gifted you, by recognising and revering the Christ-life coming to birth in you? Whom have you gifted in this way?

What 'stars' have you followed through your life? Where have they led? Where are they leading you now? What is it that keeps you going, as you follow the star of your deepest desiring and dreaming?

The magi offered the child Jesus their gifts of gold, frankincense and myrrh – symbols of kingly power, of prayer and of sorrow. What might these gifts mean to you? What brings you joy and strength? What draws you into prayer? What represents your heart's sorrow? Bring your own versions of these gifts to the Child, and tell him how you feel about them.

Joy, prayerfulness and sorrow ~ what shape do your gifts take?

The infancy of our believing

The few stories we have of the childhood of Jesus are a precious gift. They invite us to reflect on our own spiritual childhood – not as something to be 'grown out of' but as an essential stage of our becoming the people God is dreaming us to be. This infancy is something we share with the incarnate God. It is characterised by:

- the condition of helplessness, in which we were utterly dependent on others. Jesus' own helpless dependence at the beginning of his life is mirrored in the passive helplessness of Calvary, at the end.
- the presence of wonder, when everything was new and the world still undiscovered. For us, as for the Lord, this was not the naivety of youth, but the spring of life from which flows all our subsequent wonder at creation and its Creator.
- the ability to live entirely in the present moment, trusting completely in the love that carries us.
- the experience of community. There is not just a child, but a parent or family and a spirit of enfolding love. There is not just the infant Jesus, but his Father, and the enfolding love of the Holy Spirit.
- the eventual push of independence, that can be so hard to those who feel 'pushed away', but which is actually only the child pushing himself away from the harbour walls in order to swim into the oceans of his life.
- the tension between childhood obedience and the desire for in-dependent action. For Jesus this was lived out between the faithful 'hidden life' in the carpenter's family of Nazareth, and the growing sense of a mission much larger than this, and much more exposed.

To know that we share these experiences with Jesus is not just a comfort and encouragement. It is the first step along the Kingdom path, just as a baby's crawling is an essential stage in its learning to walk. Earlier in this chapter we looked through the eyes of the Trinity, down upon our teem-ing, needy world. Now Jesus is taking his own first steps in learning to walk, redemptively, through this same world. We have everything to learn from these first steps, because the journey he began is being continued in every step we take ourselves.

Read and ponder the words in Luke 2:39-40, 51-2. Allow your own childhood to be joined with the childhood of the Lord. What memories come to mind for you? Tell him, in your prayer, about your own experience of childhood helplessness, or wonder, of family or of loneliness, of the desire for independence and the desire to stay safe at home. Let him show you how these experiences were actually the first faltering steps along your Kingdom path.

Notice how you too have 'grown in stature' in your spiritual journeying over the years, and talk to the Lord about the trials and the joys of that growth.

If you have children of your own, or if you are in regular contact with small children, what do you learn from the stories of Jesus' childhood that sheds light on *their* growth and development?

One of the gifts of childhood, that we possibly only discern with hindsight, is the rather uncomfortable gift of realising that everything is *provisional*. 'Provisional' carries the double meaning of 'that which provides', and 'that which moves on'. Children trust implicitly that they will be provided with what they need (though tragically, for some, this trust is misplaced). They also accept, with an openness that we might envy, the fact that life moves on and changes day by day, and that they have little control over it all.

This basic trust, and the provisional nature of what we think of as our security, are very quickly challenged in the life of the holy family. The idyll of Bethlehem rapidly develops into the terror of exile and the horrific events they leave behind them, in the mass killings of the children of Bethlehem, at the hands of a tyrant whose spirit still stalks the world in so many modern blood-baths and 'ethnic cleansings'.

Carrying the Christ-life, and letting it 'grow in stature' in our lives, may bring us up against confrontation and hostility. For some, this may be life-threatening, and physical exile or captivity may become a reality. For most of us, at some stage, there will be a need to flee into the exile of solitude, especially while the Christ-life within us is still very young and tender. We may also be called upon to protect the newborn Christ-life in others, and take decisive, and even risk-laden, action, to guard our fellow pilgrims. As Jesus lived out his early years in the community of a human family, so we too walk the Kingdom path in the community of each other, mutually responsible for one another.

Perhaps Joseph often pondered that first dream that had assured him that all would be well with Mary and the coming child, and his own marriage intentions. Maybe he felt that that dream was turning into a nightmare far worse than even he could have imagined. And at that point there comes a new assurance, again in a dream, guiding him forward into the next step – just one next step in the darkness of trust.

Read and reflect on the story of the flight into Egypt as told in Matthew 2:13-23. Join Joseph in his anxiety, and in his trust. Talk with him, if you feel so drawn, about how you feel about the tension between fear and trust in your own life.

Listen to the news of refugees and asylum seekers in our own day. You might feel drawn to find out whether there are any refugees in your home town and if so, where they are being housed, and how they are being treated. If you are unhappy with what you find, is there anything practical you could do about it?

The threshold of adolescence

Finally we find Jesus making his own bid for independence and beginning the search for his own identity. Anyone who has brought up children will have little difficulty in relating to the story of how Jesus gets lost in Jerusalem, and how his frantic parents eventually track him down among the doctors of law in the Temple.

We can well imagine how Mary and Joseph must have felt as they set off home and then discovered that the boy was not with them. Only after a day's journey do they realise that he is not with anyone else in the pilgrimage party either. A whole three days later they discover him in the Temple. Searching for a lost child for as little as an hour is perhaps the most nerve-wracking event of a parent's experience. But to lose the Son of God for three days is something else!

But God, of course, is bigger than all our carelessness, and one lesson from this story is the importance of getting the horse before the cart. We so easily take upon ourselves a responsibility for bringing the Kingdom into being, and lose sight of our own helplessness to do anything except let God's Dream be dreamed in us. In this case, Jesus was dreaming God's Dream in a way that still lay beyond his parents' imagination. The resulting blown fuse of tension was perhaps inevitable. 'Where have you been?

We've been looking for you everywhere!' 'We've been worried sick. Why did you do this to us?'

And the calm reply – and we can read into the words whatever tone we wish – 'Why all this bother? Didn't you realise I would be in my Father's house?' Mary and Joseph experience here the pain of a tension that each of us will feel as we make the Kingdom journey – the tension between living with the demands of our 'outer' world, and the need to live true to the guiding of our 'inner' world. There is no easy compromise. For Jesus' earthly parents, the painful process of letting go has begun.

Nearly thirty years later, the whole world 'lost' the Son of God for three days, in the darkness of the tomb. The first loss marked the beginning of Jesus' sense of his personal ministry. The second loss marked the point when he passed on the continuance of that ministry to us!

Read and reflect on the story of Jesus' time in the Temple, in Luke 2:41-50. How does this incident leave you feeling? Have you ever felt the need yourself to be 'in your Father's house' – that is, engaged with your inner life, in ways that have been misunderstood by others? How do you live creatively with the tension between the obligations of your outer life and the calling of your inner life?

Perhaps you know the pain of being apparently rejected by an adolescent son or daughter who is beginning to fly the nest, yet still needs its protection. If so, you might like to talk with Mary and Joseph about how you feel. Then have the same talk with the twelve-year-old Jesus, and listen to his point of view.

The Kingdom path is taking shape. God has come down to earth, quite literally, and the pattern of his incarnation is becoming clear:

- We do well to seek him on the margins of society, not in the expected places.
- We must expect confrontation and rejection, if we travel his path.
- We need to be prepared for setbacks and even a serious backlash.
- We are urged to keep going, and growing, through all the obscurity and hidden-ness of our own lives.
- We needn't expect an easy, comfortable relationship with 'authority', either secular or religious.
- In spite of all this, the journey is the most deeply attractive calling in our lives, and it leads to joy beyond imagining.

The attraction of the
journey is stronger than
the pull of all the picnics
along the way

Just a foretaste of the nature of the journey. In the next chapter we are asked to take our 'choosing' further, in the light of all that we are discovering about the nature of the Kingdom, and its King.

5. SCANDALOUS BLESSINGS

Imagine yourself in a meeting with other Christian friends. A group of about a hundred and twenty people have gathered – not the kind of numbers to thrill the heart of a modern minister, yet from these few people – less than a typical church hall full of them – the Kingdom Story will be told all over the world. This is no fairy story. This is the first circle of 'cells' of disciples and apostles to have grown from that First Cell of the Body of Christ, Jesus himself. They have gathered together to talk over developments after the death of their Lord. These are the people with whom he first shared himself and his Truth. And we ourselves are on the growing edge of that circle today, still charged and commissioned, as they were, to tell the Kingdom Story to our generation.

But there is a gap in the circle. The Twelve are now only Eleven. One of the 'cells', Judas, has betrayed the Kingdom, and has become eternally separated, by his own choice, from the circle of the Body of Christ. A new person is needed, to fill that gap and complete the circle. Peter explains the situation to the gathered followers of the Lord, and he even gives them a job description! The person they are looking for will be someone who has been 'with us the whole time that the Lord Jesus was living with us, from the time when John was baptising until the day when he was taken up from us…to serve with us as a witness to his resurrection' (Acts 1:21-2). The fledgling apostle will be one who knows Jesus intimately (not just someone who knows *about* him), and who has made the Kingdom journey alongside him through his earthly ministry. It will be a person whose life bears witness to Jesus' resurrected presence and power. And there will always be a gap in the circle, until the Kingdom comes and we are all brought home into our one-ness in the heart of God. This 'twelfth person' is continually being sought, in every generation, and in every new day, and every hour of every day. We are all called to be Number Twelve. Are *you* going to apply?

The question is a nonsense, of course. Because the call to be a Kingdom-builder doesn't come in response to our 'application'. The initiative is always with God. All we can do is respond. Or fail to respond. (And indeed, these first apostles went on, during that meeting, to ask God to make the decision for them.) Nevertheless, you *have* responded to the Call of the King in your own life and you have weighed some of the consequences of that call. You have consented to God's coming to birth in your own life. How do you feel now that you have read and considered the 'job description' for the Kingdom Venture? Remember its main features:

- To know the Lord intimately.
- To have been with him through his earthly ministry, from the start, when he was baptised by John, through to his ascension.
- To be a living witness to the presence and the power of his resurrected life.

Called to be Number Twelve ?

Is it an impossible demand? Or might the Kingdom journey be leading you to just that place? A place where, through your prayer, you are coming to know the Lord intimately, as a friend. A meditative journey through the Gospel narratives, which is inviting you to be present to every aspect of Jesus' lived ministry. And a transforming experience of his love that is forming you into a living presence of his resurrected life in your generation.

You have already shared in the story of Jesus' early years, and the trials that his earthly parents went through. You have explored some of the connections between this story and your own personal story, and seen the beginnings of what the Kingdom journey is like. The signs are not, on the surface, immediately attractive. Notably lacking from the picture are features like 'comfort', 'satisfaction', 'ease', 'wealth', 'power' and 'status'.

Yet you are still here! You haven't dismissed the whole project as a hiding to nothing. In fact you have accepted and embraced the call to follow Christ and to let your own life become a specific and particular expression of the incarnation. The road now leads on:

- through the *discipleship*, of learning all that the Lord longs to teach you,
- to the apostolate, of being sent out into the world to tell the Kingdom Story in your own life.

Imagine yourself present to that early meeting of the disciples and apostles, as they discuss what it means to be an apostle, and what is required of such a person. How do you feel when the gaze falls upon *you*? Do you want to make a journey of prayer in intimate friendship with the Lord, as they did? Make your response to God in whatever way feels right for you.

The leaving of Nazareth

A poignant song that was in the charts some years ago put the small cathedral town of Durham in north-east England on the map of popular culture. It was called 'The leaving of Durham Town' and it expressed the feelings of someone who has to leave the place they call home, to venture out into the wider world, to earn a livelihood and forge a new direction in life.

This experience comes to everyone in some form, as life moves on, and we have to leave behind a phase of our lives that we have grown through, to move on to the uncharted territory of the next stage of our living. For most of us, the transition is not accomplished without pain, and a degree of fear about all that lies ahead. But there is excitement too, especially if we have freely chosen to take this next step.

My own most recent experience of these feelings was just a few weeks ago, when I left my job and, indeed, left the 'work force' for good. It was my own decision. I had freely chosen to resign my job in industry and 'cast myself on the waters' for the years that still stretched out between me and my pension. I wanted to do it and I looked forward to my last working day. However, when that day actually came, I was surprised to find that there was a lot of regret and ambivalence in my heart. Walking away from my colleagues for the last time wasn't as easy as I had thought. Cutting myself off from the comfortable identity of 'one of the work force' after over thirty years turned out to be quite a challenge to my sense of security – emotional as well as financial. My colleagues gave me a great send-off, and I had to work hard to keep back the tears. Then I walked away, and into a whole new, and still very uncertain phase of my life.

When I took these feelings into prayer, I found myself, in imagination, at Nazareth, watching Jesus leave home to begin his public life. I could feel something of his own anxiety, as he walked away from Nazareth, aware of the sight of his home and family receding into the background, and with only the vaguest notion of all that might lie ahead of him. Then I felt with Mary her sense of loss as her son walked away into an uncertain future.

Eventually, I felt Jesus come alongside me, in our shared 'walking away'. I heard his promise 'I am with you always', but it was coupled with a thrilling invitation: 'Journey with me, as my apprentice. Experience, along-side me, everything that happens, in Galilee, and in Jerusalem. Learn from me, by watching me in action and listening to all I say. We are "on the road" together. I am the Master, and you are the apprentice. There won't be any permanent resting places, or anywhere that we can finally call "home", but the Way will be our home from now on.'

And if you feel, as I do, a little on the elderly side for taking on an apprenticeship like this, be reassured – your soul will stretch to encompass the miles, and God will never force you further than you freely choose to go.

Risking life beyond the comfort zone

Sometimes the call to move on to a new phase of our lives comes upon us with a jolt, through some unexpected event or challenge. The panic we feel when this happens can make us defensive, tempting us to deny the challenge and remain safely in our 'comfort zone'. If we do, we may miss out on an opportunity for radical transformation. Jesus encounters this experience during a wedding party . . .

Read and reflect on the story of the Wedding at Cana, in John 2:1-12. Try to enter the scene in your imagination. Who is there at the party? Where do you find yourself? How do you feel? Notice how events unfold. Listen to Mary's comment, that the wine has run out, and to Jesus' reaction. It is a pivotal moment, not only for the wedding guests, but for Jesus himself. He hears the challenge, to exercise his power in a new way. Does the story bring back any memories of pivotal moments in your own life, when you realised you were standing on the threshold of something new, and frightening? Let events proceed. Listen to Mary's advice: 'Do as he tells you.' What happens? Notice the empty vessels. Let them be filled. Let them be transformed. Let them be poured out. Is there anything you feel you want to say to Jesus? Can you end your prayer with the words of the annunciation:'Let what you have said be done to me!'?

Grace descending . . .

The celebration of the Lord's baptism is something very close to my own heart. Many years ago, after I had wandered for years in a wilderness of personal confusion, I felt an urgent need to search for the God I had once known, but appeared to have lost. Tentatively, and tearfully, I made my way back to the nearest Christian community I knew of, where to my amazement and relief, I was welcomed, listened to, and accepted, just as I was. I thank God every day that I live for this experience.

The person who welcomed me that morning extended an invitation to me: 'to come back into communion, and into community'. With great trepidation I went back to that church two weeks later. It was the feast of the baptism of the Lord, and I felt as though I too had been to the depths of the Jordan, and been lifted out again by God himself. Now, every year when this feast is celebrated, I relive my own experience of those depths – in which I had truly felt that my soul was drowning. And then I relive that moment of being lifted out of the chaos of my inner whirlpools, and I hear the voice that John the Baptist heard:'*This is my Son, the Beloved. My grace rests on him! Let him touch your own troubled heart with that grace.*'

Something of the presence of that dove of peace that flew across the Jordan descended on me during that period of my life. I know now that God heard my inarticulate cry for help, and that he reached down to restore me into the bond of his covenant love from which I had so dangerously strayed.

Peace out of storm clouds... new beginnings out of darkest depths

---

Read and reflect on the story of Jesus' baptism, in Matthew 3:1-17. Notice any part of the narrative that especially holds your attention, and ponder that part in depth. Does the incident remind you of anything in your own life? Have you ever experienced the depths of your own helplessness, perhaps, or known moments when the peace of God seemed to descend on you quite undeservedly?

Remember in your prayer your own special moments of commitment, perhaps in adult baptism or confirmation, or in an act of reconciliation which restored you into right relationship with God, yourself and the world. Express your feelings about such moments to God in your prayer, and perhaps to a soul-friend.

Voices in the desert

Where there is grace, temptation is never far away. When God's action in our lives appears to be most powerful and visible, that is often precisely the time when we experience the greatest pull from all the negative counter-forces. It is not uncommon for people who are about to commit themselves to some work or ministry that has the potential to change lives, to find themselves beset by every kind of setback, ranging from broken-down cars, to family turmoil or illness, or, most destructively of all, their own inner wavering. You have probably already discovered this dynamic for yourself.

But we are on an apprentice journey. Let's accompany Jesus now beyond the grace and affirmation of his baptism, straight into the desert, where he went to pray, but where 'the devil' (however we may understand that term) was waiting for him. The Gospel accounts reveal this episode in the desert as a 'one-off' experience for Jesus. For us, however, it is a continual state. Learning to notice when we are being pulled off course, and to understand the nature of those forces that are doing the pulling, is the first huge lesson of our apprenticeship with the Lord.

The account of Jesus' temptations gives us a wonderfully succinct introduction to the nature of the negative impulses that work against the True Life we are seeking to live. We see Jesus himself struggling with the deep and disturbing questions that haunt us day by day, and seeking to steer a course of truth through an ocean of falsehood. In the desert, he faces, head on, the destructive movements that are part and parcel of what it means to be human. The importance of recognising these destructive movements within and around us, and taking steps to act against them, is crucial to our growth into the Reign of God. Before we look at how Jesus handled the onslaught of the negative forces around him, we might take a little time to reflect on what is going on in ourselves, and how we are handling it at present.

Just as God is calling each of us to become a living presence of himself and his love in his creation, there is an almost equally powerful counter-force trying to enlist us, as it were, 'on the opposite side'. This opposite polarity constantly seeks to turn our lives into embodiments of the many false values of what we might call 'the opposite kingdom'. It was this 'opposite polarity' that Jesus was wrestling with in the desert.

Traditionally these two opposing spiritual polarities have been called 'God' and 'Satan', or 'good' and 'evil'. It is easy to convince ourselves that we have made our choice for God, and thereby become immune to the destructive forces around us. This wasn't true for Jesus. It isn't true for us. This misplaced confidence can be challenged if we think of the two polarities in terms of *movements*, rather than as some kind of absolute condition of 'good' or 'evil'.

These movements are everywhere: in our social and economic structures, in the Church, and in the most secret recesses of our own hopes and fears. There are movements in all of these situations that are positive and creative. If we live in line with their flow, and allow them to draw us on, we will be furthering the Kingdom of God. And there are movements that are negative and destructive. If we allow these to pull us into their currents, we will become, however unwittingly, agents of kingdoms alien to the Reign of God. The process is one of continual flux. But it is a process of *choice*, not chance. In everything that happens to us, and in every interaction with the world around us, and with its institutions, we need to be continually asking:

- Is this movement coming from God? Is it creative? Is it furthering the Reign of God?
- Or is this movement undermining the Reign of God? Is it coming from a source that is ultimately destructive?

Once these questions are programmed into our living, a deeper range of choosing opens up for us:

- Do I choose to go along with the drawing of the creative movements in my living, or to neglect them?
- Do I choose to follow the negative, destructive movements in my living, or to act against them?

In any one day, all of us will experience many different movements like these, both negative and positive, and we will sometimes choose wisely, sometimes not.

Recognising the inner movements

We have made our choice for the Kingdom. We have chosen deep down to follow the Call of the King. Because of this fundamental 'bedrock' choice, two things follow:

- When we are choosing in line with the creative pull within us, the pull of God, we will experience a sense of 'rightness' – a serenity in the core of our being, which we can trust, even if the surface layers of ourselves are in a state of turbulence.
- When we are choosing in a way that does not align with the 'true north' registered by our inner compass, we will feel the turmoil in the core of our being – even though we may be fairly satisfied with ourselves and the world at the surface levels of our living.

How wonderful, if it were so simple! In practice, of course, the deeper reasons for our feelings of 'rightness' or 'wrongness', of 'peace' or 'dis-ease' may be very far from obvious. We may feel disturbed when we are reflecting on a particular matter, but the root cause of that disturbance may lie quite elsewhere. For example, I may meet a neighbour in the street one morning, and find myself feeling irritated at the delay she is causing in my schedule, and impatient with her as she tells me more than I wanted to know about her present state of health. But do these disgruntled and rather disturbing feelings have anything at all to do with my neighbour? Perhaps they are indicating some deeper discontent with my own sense of being time-driven all the time. Or they may be nudging into some unacknowledged fear of illness that her comments have awakened in me. A crucial part of the process of discernment, therefore, is to seek to recognise the *roots* of our feelings and reactions, and to do so in prayer, asking God to guide us.

When we have reached some degree of understanding about the deeper roots of what we are feeling and doing, a further question opens up: Which do I desire *more*:

- the deep sense of peace and at-one-ness with God and my true self, at the core of my being (even if this means living through a great deal of turbulence, hardship and loss, at the outer layers of my living)
- or the maintenance of relative peace, comfort and security in the outer layers of my life, even though this may be gained at the cost of unease and diminishment in the deeper reaches of my being?

Ultimately, the choice in favour of deep peace at the core of our being leads to inner *freedom* – a freedom from the need to service continually the demands of our 'outer layers', and our constant anxieties about the future, about our popularity ratings, and so on. The choice in favour of the relative peace in the outer layers leaves us *enslaved* to everything that causes those anxieties: the need for more money to comfort ourselves with more possessions and surround ourselves with more security or the need to strive for status and affirmation.

Discernment is about the process of registering these movements. A good way to discern the movements going on in us, day by day, is to spend a little while each day simply noticing the day's events and how we feel the movements within us were through these events and interactions. The 'Review of the Day' prayer, outlined in Chapter 2, is a great help in doing this kind of reflection. It is a way of reading our 'inner compass', and noticing when we felt we were 'living true' and when we felt we were going 'off course'. The turbulence in our hearts will give us warning when we are going off course, relative to the deepest core of our being, where God is indwelling.

However, the process of discernment is not always easy, and it is an ongoing challenge, moment by moment. If you would like to go into it more deeply, you might find the companion book *Landmarks* a help in learning to read the movements of your heart more sensitively, and in exploring more fully the root causes of these movements and the implications of personal truth and inner freedom.

Caterpillars and butterflies

Once we have become familiar with the process of noticing our inner movements, how do we ensure that we really do opt for what is positive, and work against what is negative? Of course, this is the work not of a week or a year, but of a lifetime. Nor can it be learned from a book, but only in the deepening life with God in our prayer and our daily living.

The way that helps me most is to keep constantly in mind that there will frequently be a discrepancy between what is happening at the core of my being, and what is happening on the outer layers. This helps me to focus on what the core of my being is saying and registering, and to attach less importance to what the outer layers are shouting about. Unfortunately 'shouting' is exactly what they do, and it isn't at all easy to hear the quiet stirrings at the core of our being, through all the loud clamouring on the outer edges. I may feel very sure that the deep core of myself is really looking for the Reign of God, and desires, above all, to be engaged, whole-heartedly, in the process of the coming of the Kingdom. But the outer layers of myself are much more concerned with keeping me comfortable, well fed, secure, and well thought of.

The whole picture reminds me of a caterpillar. Caterpillars, like most creatures, are only concerned with two matters:

- to grow into bigger and bigger caterpillars, by munching their way through every leaf that turns up
- and to protect themselves against anything that threatens that process, perhaps by turning into the colour of what they eat, to conceal them-selves, or by growing bristles to deter any attacker.

My own outer layers are very much like that. I want to grow and expand into more and more of 'myself' (that is, my 'ego-self'), I want to make my mark on the world, and I defend myself, often quite unnecessarily and unreasonably, against all perceived threats, and especially against the ulti-mate threat of death. My life starts to resemble the environment I am attached to. I take on the 'colours' of my world.

But a caterpillar changes, and becomes a chrysalis. It hangs, apparently lifeless, but in fact expending huge energy – the energy of transformation. Because deep in the core of the caterpillar is a butterfly! I believe that there is a 'butterfly' reality deep in the core of all our caterpillar living. The secret of discernment seems to have something to do with registering when we are following the clamour of the greedy caterpillar in our outer layers, and when we are responding to our true 'butterfly' self waiting for birth into an eternal realm of being.

To reach this kind of transformation, we may have to let go of all that we valued as caterpillars – those luscious leaves, and those efficient defence systems – and allow our 'ego-selves' apparently to 'die' and hang like a lifeless, passive cocoon – a meagre, fragile shelter for our growing inner butterfly. But this 'dying' is actually a gateway to resurrection, and to the emergence of a whole new state of being – breathtakingly beautiful, and free.

If we go back now to the two poles or force fields that operate in our lives – the negative and the positive, the destructive and the creative – we begin to see that:

Believing in transformation?
'You'll never get me up in
one of those contraptions!'

- the negative pull is trying to persuade us to stay as caterpillars. It wants us to use our energy and imagination and giftedness just to grow into bigger, more impressive, well-defended, invulnerable caterpillars who have the power to ensure that we get at least our own share of life's cake, if not a bit more. It wants to keep us enslaved in this way of being.
- the positive, or creative pull is fighting for our freedom to be who we

really are. It is suggesting, continually, that there is something infinitely more precious at the core of our being, but that to liberate this eternal reality we have to let go of what we think – in our caterpillar existence – is essential to our well-being and happiness.

And this conflict is going on in every moment. Sometimes it will be obvious: Do I choose to buy an extra cake or to give the money to the homeless man sitting on the side of the road? But far more frequently the choosing will be very subtle indeed. To learn to notice when we are being affected by which kind of movement, and to respond from the core of our being, rather than from the outside edges, we will need a wise guide along-side us. Jesus is the only guide we can trust, through the gift of his Spirit. To make the Kingdom journey as his disciple is, above all, a way of learning to choose for Life in every little thing we do.

Look back over your day. In what ways were you operating from your 'caterpillar' self? In what ways were you responding to the 'butterfly'?

But there is another factor that encourages me tremendously, when I reflect on the magnitude of the task of choosing what leads me closer to God in any specific matter. God, I am convinced, holds a preferential option for Life, and God (so a friend, who is also a master of under-statement, once reminded me) is not easily undermined!

God's preferential option for Life

At the beginning of this journey we reflected on the fact that we are 'like a grain of dust that tips the scales'. A grain of dust – very small, transient and insignificant in our 'ego-selves', but with the potential, deep in the core of our being, where our true self is at one with God, to 'tip the scales', either in favour of Life or in opposition to Life.

We also reflected on that primeval struggle between the mutually destructive particles and anti-particles. Only a tiny imbalance of matter over anti-matter permitted creation to evolve. The difference was infinitesimal – just the ninth decimal place of one per cent. This is scientific fact. But it is also, for me, a revelation of the reality of God.

This source of all, this God, to whom I desire to commit myself, has, from the very beginning of time and space, operated a policy of positive dis-crimination in favour of Life. This preferential option is written into the laws that govern the universe. And I believe it is also written into our personal struggles to choose in favour of Life in the day-to-day choices that we face throughout our lives. Often the margin will be very small indeed, and sometimes our choices against Life and the Kingdom values will seem to be winning, but at the end of the day, Life will always win the struggle.

We can see this dynamic operating in all kinds of ways, just by keeping our eyes open as we go about our daily living. We can see the difference between choosing from the core of our being, for the butterfly rather than the caterpillar. And we can see the effects of making choices according to the values of the caterpillar.

Perhaps, for example, you have worked for years on end to train for a particular job. Or you may have given the best years of your life to the task of bringing up children through all kinds of crises, cost, and drains on your energy. Perhaps you have stayed in touch with a friend through thick and thin, even in spite of hostility and rejection? On the face of it, these choices were not immediately rewarding. They didn't serve the caterpillar king-dom. They didn't bring you any comfort, or security. On the contrary, you even took on board some considerable discomfort, inconvenience, cost and vulnerability. Why did you stay with these things? What kept you going?

The word 'attraction' springs to mind. At the core of your being, you were living in the deeply attractive magnetic field of the 'butterfly' – your true self, your Godself. The desire to do and become what you knew you had the potential to do or become kept you going through long years of training. The desire to nurture another human life into the realisation of its potential kept you going through all the trials of parenting. The desire to be a faithful friend kept you going through the dark patches of a relationship. Truly, there is energy in our desires, when they are rooted in the core of our being. There is enough energy to turn our caterpillar selves into butterflies of Life.

At the heart of the matter, the core of our being knows that the end is worth the means. It has this wisdom because it is at one with the bedrock reality of God, where all creation is held in wholeness and interrelatedness. When our choices are coming from the core of our being, we know that we are living true, and we are even able and willing to face a great deal of hardship if that is what it takes to live by the Kingdom Dream.

The negative force fields work in the opposite direction. They tempt us to give up on something because it is too demanding, or to neglect to speak out on an important issue, because to do so might make others laugh at us. They seduce us into believing that we need to surround ourselves with complex security systems, both externally, and in our relationships. They encourage us to cushion ourselves and to take what we need for this process from those around us. They feed our fantasies that we must have personal status, popularity and recognition in order to have any identity or value. We can get sucked into their eddies as individuals, tribes and families, as cliques and clubs, as multi-national companies, as nation states and even as 'Church'.

What makes us choose in ways that deny the Kingdom values we so long to embody in our lives? The answer seems to have a lot to do with *fear*. And fear comes from the deep insecurity of living our lives as if we were autonomous 'islands', each of us potentially threatened by the others, and exploiting or abusing the others to protect our own dominion. It is the first sin of Adam and Eve again, and it doesn't show much sign of going away.

The true story that follows is about a struggle between the negative and the positive force fields. It demonstrates how the butterfly wins out over the drag of the caterpillar, with transforming power.

The Candy Bomber

In 1948 there was an international incident . . .

After the Second World War, Germany was divided into four zones of occupation: American, French, British and Soviet. Berlin, the capital city, was in the middle of the Soviet-occupied zone and also divided into the same four zones of occupation. The result was the little pocket of West Berlin in the middle of what was to become Eastern Germany – over a hundred miles east of the rest of West Germany. The only access routes for supplies to its two million inhabitants were the land routes between West Berlin and West Germany, and three air corridors. In 1948 the Soviets suddenly closed all the land connections. Only the air corridors remained viable. The Berliners woke one morning to find they were under siege. The blockade of the city had begun. This episode in history was explored in a TV documentary.

Against this backdrop, let's eavesdrop now on a high level meeting to discuss the situation. Imagine the scene. The war had only been over for a couple of years, and the anger and distrust between Germany and the allies was still very raw and real. There was no love lost for the besieged Berliners. The meeting might have ended in stalemate, had it not been for one bold voice who suggested: 'I just wonder whether it might be feasible to keep the city supplied just using the air routes . . .?' The question wasn't taken too seriously at first. But the questioner persisted. He was thinking on his feet, working out the mathematics of the situation. 'I really think it might just be possible,' he continued, as he set out his calculations to his colleagues. Interest gradually flickered to life around the room. It became, first, a technical challenge. 'Perhaps we really *could* do it.' And then a moral challenge: 'Perhaps we *should* try it.' And finally, it ignited a flame of enthusiasm and idealism: '*Let's go for it!*'

And so began the Berlin Air Lift – a bold and dramatic rescue operation to supply the daily needs of two million people using a fleet of aircraft and three inadequate landing strips in the beleaguered city, in the teeth of the waiting Soviet army. It was a modern-day David taking on an apparently invincible Goliath.

Men who had only a few months previously been flying bombing raids over Berlin, with the deliberate intention of destroying its buildings and killing its people, were now asked to fly a mercy mission to supply these same people with food and with the means to rebuild the city. It was a nose-to-tail exercise, with aircraft landing and taking off every three minutes, and it was sustained for fourteen months, non-stop, until the blockades were lifted. And it was dangerous. Over seventy of the pilots lost their lives.

One of the pilots became something of a legend in Berlin. He got the idea of making little packs of candy, with whatever post-war sweets he could get, and attaching these parcels to tiny parachutes. Then, breaking all the rules, he would open a hatch as he flew in over the city, and drop his own little air-lift offerings for the children waiting along the flight path below. They called him the Candy Bomber, and his arrival was greeted every time by a sea of upturned faces as hundreds of excited and expectant children waited for their hero to let his blessings fall upon them.

At the end of the TV programme, two people were interviewed. One was an elderly German man who had been a schoolboy in 1948. In a voice still quivering with emotion, he spoke of how profoundly the action of the air-lift pilots had influenced and inspired the people of Berlin. The other was one of the allied pilots, now a veteran. He vehemently deflected any credit for the action. The heroes of the day, he said, had been the people of Berlin, who had simply refused ever to surrender to the despair of the times, and whose buoyancy had carried the whole action through to success.

For me, this story demonstrates the creative pull of God in action. It reveals the very dynamic of God who is continually drawing us towards the more creative route, in every detail of our lived experience:

> *Taking our 'bad', and moving it to 'good', to 'better', to 'best'.*

Against this, the pull of the destructive movements works in the opposite direction, taking our 'good' and dragging it down to 'poor' and to 'worst'.

The Candy Bomber grew up in the early Forties, when the destructive dynamic was dragging the whole of Europe down from good to bad, and from bad to worse.

- Beginning from a reasonably civilised society in Europe between the wars, fear starts to stalk the streets. Fear of unemployment. Fear of hunger. Fear of the people next door, the country on our borders.
- Good degenerates (with horrifying speed) to the Bad of open conflict. Ordinary men and women are trained into efficient killers, raining death on civilians trapped in 'enemy' towns and cities.
- The Bad of war spirals down into the Worst of hatred and distrust sown in individual human hearts, fed by the propaganda machine to believe that men and women who happen to live in a different country and speak a different language are sub-human and fit targets for mass destruction.

Now watch the opposite dynamic in action – the dynamic of Love and of God.

- The word goes out that two million people are under siege, and will die of starvation unless something drastic can be done to save them. This is the Bad of the beginning.
- Then comes the 'good' – the idea that just possibly they might be saved by air. People's imaginations are fired, and the desire to do this good thing begins to dispel their doubts about the former 'enemy'.

- They start to put all their energy into the task of implementing this vision. They have reached the 'better'. After fourteen months of non-stop flights and courageous determination the blockade is lifted and Berlin is free again.
- And finally the 'best'. Read again the comments of the two veterans in the programme. See how the dynamic of Love has transformed the 'worst' of total war into the 'best' of mutual admiration and respect. The scales have been tipped resoundingly and Love has been vindicated.

Can you see any events in your life that seemed destructive at the time, but now reveal a movement that seems to have drawn good out of bad? Can you see any areas of your life where the opposite movement seems to have happened, and, as a result of your own or other people's fears, something good has degenerated into a less good, or a bad situation?

Just notice these movements in your life, without judgement either of yourself or of others. Thank God for all that is moving from bad to good to better, and ask his healing and light upon anything that seems to be moving from bad to worse.

Forty nights on the mountain

Our apprentice journey with the Lord brings us to the point where he himself struggled against the destructive forces we have been exploring. Let's place ourselves alongside him on the mountainside and hear what the tempter has to say.

First: 'You are a human being with human needs. You are hungry. There is nothing sinful about feeling hungry. Everyone needs to eat. Why not take these stones here and turn them into bread? You know you can do it.'

There is, indeed, nothing wrong in feeling human hunger and satisfying it with human bread. So why does Jesus refuse? Perhaps the reason lies in that searching question: 'In this particular situation, what course of action is leading me closer to the deep purpose at the core of my being?' He is fasting, and trying to discern the direction of his ministry. This temptation to retreat back into the comfort zone is not the best way to move forward. 'Bread isn't the number one priority,' he replies. 'Human hearts need the word of God even more than human bodies need bread.'

Second: 'You can prove that you are the Son of God. You don't need to put yourself through all this weary walking and ministering to people who won't listen to what you tell them. The angels will protect you in everything you do, so force the people to recognise you for who you are. Leap off this cliff and prove you are divine.'

Have we not sometimes wished ourselves that God would pull out the trump card and turn people's hearts to him by some spectacular coup? But Jesus knows there is no short cut to transformation. He is the Lord of the journey, whose love and power have to be *discovered* by those prepared to journey with him. The journey will pass through dark and dangerous places, but ultimate security lies in travelling with God. The compelling miracle is to be set aside, in favour of a journey of trust.

Third: 'Everything you can see from the top of the highest mountain can be yours. You can establish your Kingdom for as far as the eye can see. Give up this nonsense about transforming people's hearts, and you can have the whole world in which to set up your Reign. You can be King of all you survey and govern everyone in your own way.'

The final temptation – to be a good king, and an all-powerful ruler, but only of the 'caterpillar world'. How tempting, and how horribly easy it is, to settle for 'living a good life' and 'being a good Christian', but only on our own little island world, in orbit round our own centre of gravity! 'No!' says the Lord. 'The centre of gravity is God and God alone.'

Read and reflect on the story of Jesus' time of temptation, in Matthew 4: 1-11. What light does it shed on your own tendencies? Imagine the tempter talking to *you*. What do you think he might say to you, to distract you from the deep desire at the core of your being? In what ways are you tempted to short cut or block off the journey of discovery of your true self?

A scandalous blessing

So there is no short cut to wholeness. And there are no compromises. Like the girl who claimed that she was 'only a little bit pregnant', to say that we are living good Christian lives, and leave it at that, is falling far short of the truth. The way of God is an all or nothing affair. It upturns all reasonable human expectations. It challenges us to become fools in the eyes of the world. But in its scandalous demands, it bestows the one true blessing that our souls long for and the world hungers after.

Jesus embarks on his public ministry on another hillside, this time near Capernaum – and delivers his manifesto. It doesn't have the makings of a vote-catching exercise. It certainly wouldn't get past today's PR men and spin doctors. But here we are, two thousand years on, still praying with it, reflecting on it, and even trying to live by it. Even those who were never inside a church have heard of the Sermon on the Mount. What's the secret?

The secret is surely that Jesus' manifesto is offering a way of life lived under an entirely different standard to that of any earthly kingdom or political or social system. Listen to some of its terms:

- The defenceless, the oppressed and those with no standing are the lucky ones: they are closer to becoming butterflies and flying free of their oppressors.
- The gentle people are the ones to emulate. They have a power within themselves that far outweighs all the force and violence in human nature.
- Those who are grief-stricken and living in the shadow of loss and sorrow have every reason to be joyful, because their sorrow is deepening the channels of grace in their hearts.
- The campaigners and strugglers for peace and justice should rejoice, because what they are striving for is what the Reign of God is all about.
- Those who take pity on others and show them mercy have an inner freedom and strength that is denied to the forceful, the vengeful and those who wield power.
- The ones who acknowledge the emptiness inside them, without trying to fill it, are privileged indeed, because they will discover the very heart of God beating in their emptiness.
- Those who make peace are more powerful than those who wage war, because God himself is living his Dream in their lives.
- Those very people who are oppressed and tortured for maintaining their own integrity have cause for joy, because they are the honoured citizens of the Kingdom of God.
- And you? You too are blessed in the very places you would run miles to avoid! You are most to be respected when you are being abused and persecuted. Your truth shines brightest when you are being wrongly accused. You are richest of all when you have nothing left to lose. You are free when nothing enslaves you any more in the caterpillar kingdom.

Read and ponder the words of the Sermon on the Mount, in Matthew 5:1-12. Sit at the feet of Jesus as he delivers this radical call to the Kingdom Standard. Talk to him especially about any part of it that troubles you, inspires you, angers or delights you. Ask him to explain, to you personally, anything that puzzles you. How do you feel about it now? Is this really the man you want to follow?

Jesus stands there, in the wide, free world of the Kingdom, where the seeds of transformation are growing, and calls you out of the enslaving limits of your comfort zone. You have heard something of what he values, and of how the Kingdom of God is going to be. On the face of it there is every reason to say, 'Thank you, but no thank you.' But look into this man's eyes. Notice the movements of that magnetic core deep in your being. Then make your response to his call.

6. COME AND SEE

The words of the title remind me of any number of times when I have got lost in some unfamiliar place and stopped to ask someone for directions. There is some crucial bit of my brain missing – the bit that deals with maps, directions, knitting patterns and washing machine instructions. So when this happens, I listen very carefully, sometimes even to a second iteration, then I nod wisely and express my gratitude and manage a few more yards in the direction indicated, before I get lost again. Just occasionally a miracle happens. I stop to ask directions from someone who seems to understand what I really need. 'I'm going that way,' the person smiles cheerfully. 'Come with me.'

Our apprentice journey with Jesus continues with a moment like that. Here we are, ready to go, having chosen to follow this man in spite of all the indications that this will not be a journey of comfort and ease. Now where? And how? Starting from the here and now, in all the givenness of our life situations and existing commitments, just what does it mean to hear, and respond to, Jesus' call to 'Follow me'? His answer doesn't come in the shape of a shelf of books, or a canon of directives, or a course on theology, in which many of us would most certainly lose ourselves. Instead, he says: 'Come with me, and see for yourself.'

A personal calling

The Gospels relate how Jesus called a number of different people to follow him and make the apprentice journey with him. Each calling was unique, and from each there is something to learn about what it will mean to be his disciple.

I remember one summer morning when I was walking along the quay-side of a small fishing village in North-east Scotland where part of my family originated. I found myself listening to the shouted conversations between the fishermen, who were mending their nets there and attending to their boats, as I tried to make sense of the broad Buchanie dialect of the region. Then I caught myself wondering how these men would have reacted if Jesus had walked among them, invited them to drop everything and follow him. At first the prospect seemed laughable. I could well imagine the robust replies such an invitation might have called forth. But then I thought to myself: if the attraction of this man Jesus remains still so powerful across two millennia, how much more compelling must it have been on the shores of Galilee, face to face, hand to hand?

But the reality of Jesus' call to the fishermen of Galilee took on a whole new dimension one Sunday as I listened to a sermon by a visiting minister to our community, who pointed out that Jesus' call was, as he put it, 'case-specific'. He called the fishermen to follow him, in order to do a different

What might the Fisherman
say to you?

kind of fishing – fishing for the minds and hearts of their fellow men and women. Most of us, however, are not fishermen. The visiting preacher went on to invite us to reflect on what, exactly, Jesus might have said to *us*. At once my imagination ran off with me. To the teachers I could imagine him saying: 'I'll give you something eternal to teach', to the lawyers, 'I'll show you a new kind of justice', to the housewives and house-husbands, 'I'll help you to make a home where God himself may dwell', to the nurses and doctors, 'I'll teach you how to heal hearts and souls', to the journalists and media people, 'I'll give you a different kind of News to report', and to the unemployed, 'I'll teach you how Being is more important than Doing'. At the time I was working in industry as a technical author, and to me I heard him say, 'Come on, Margaret. I'll give you something worthwhile to write about!'

Read and reflect on the call of the first disciples, in Matthew 4:18-22. Try to imagine yourself in that scene. How do you feel? What do you see and hear? Notice the faces of the fishermen, and that of Jesus. Notice their first reaction, and their moment of decision. Now let Jesus approach you. Bearing in mind whatever your own main occupation is, or where your giftedness lies, what do you think Jesus would have said to *you*?

We don't, however, need any CV or previous experience or employer's references to be welcomed onto the Kingdom journey. Jesus seems to have little concern for whether or not we have anything to bring to the service of the Kingdom. On the contrary, he goes out of his way to call several people, by name, who would appear, at first sight, to be very bad news indeed.

Take Matthew, for example, who describes his own personal calling. Matthew was a tax-man – one of the people the population particularly loved to hate, a man who was working hand in hand with the occupying Roman authorities. Jesus not only calls him into a special relationship as a disciple, but stays for a meal with him and attracts other tax collectors to the table. Very soon there is a veritable taxman's party going on, with Jesus in the midst of it.

In Mark's and Luke's Gospel, Matthew's call becomes the call of Levi, a tax collector, and again, Levi's house becomes the venue for a gathering of 'tax collectors and sinners'. When Jesus is reproached for the company he keeps, he replies: 'It's not the healthy who need a doctor, but the sick. I didn't come to call the upright, but the sinners.'

Another tax collector turns up in Luke's Gospel. He is small and rich. So small that he needs to climb a tree to catch a glimpse of Jesus as he passes by among the crowds. So rich, that he has undoubtedly lined his pockets at the expense of his fellow citizens. Jesus draws him out of his obscurity dramatically, by stopping right below the tree and telling Zacchaeus that he intends to dine with him that night! Zacchaeus' amazement is matched only by that of the crowd, who mutter disapprovingly about this man who goes 'to stay at a sinner's house'.

So, if we thought it was a sign of special favour that we feel ourselves called to follow the Lord, we can rest assured that we have been chosen not for our abilities, but on account of our need.

Read the accounts of the call of Matthew (Matthew 9:9-13), Levi (Luke 5:27-32) and Zacchaeus (Luke 19:1-10). Try to imagine yourself present to the scene. Notice where you find yourself, and how you feel.

Suppose Jesus were to walk through the streets of your home town today. What groups of 'tax collectors' do you think he might especially seek out, as those most in need of blessing and healing? What class of people do your fellow citizens most look down on and despise? Where would Jesus go today, to cause the maximum scandal, do you think? Imagine him doing just that. Where do you find yourself in the scene? How do you feel now? Is there anything you want to say to him, or to those he is calling to his side?

The final personal calling we might observe happens when two of the disciples of John the Baptist see Jesus passing by, and hear John's cry of recognition: 'Behold, the lamb of God.' The two follow Jesus, not quite knowing what it is they are looking for or where they are going (feelings that most of us can relate to). Jesus turns round and asks them a simple question: 'What do you want?' But they don't know what they want. Instead, they try to change the subject: 'Where do you live, Rabbi?' – a question pregnant with undertones: 'Who are you really? What are you about? What makes you tick?' He reads their unspoken thoughts. He recognises their disorientation, and their deep desire to follow. Like the friendly person from whom I asked directions in my lost-ness, he replies with the one answer that can really respond to their need: 'Come and see!'

Read the story of this encounter for yourself, in John 1:35-9, and let yourself be present to the scene. Listen to the words of recognition: This is the lamb of God. What do you want to do when you hear this? Let your imagination play out the remainder of the scene in whatever way feels right for you.

Allow Jesus to ask you the question: 'What do you want?' Imagine him coming into your room today, and sitting down beside you, and repeating the question: 'From all that is going on in your life right now, and out of all your hopes and dreams, what would you most like me to do for you?' Give him your response, taking as long as you need, to ponder what you want to say. He is waiting to draw you forward into the Way of his Dream for you, and your own deepest dream for yourself. Hear his invitation *'Come and see.'* Set out on the journey of discovery alongside him when you feel ready, and let it lead you where it will.

'Needed on voyage'

Paddington Bear carries a big suitcase on his travels, and on this suitcase is the label saying 'Needed on voyage'. We are about to set out on a life-long journey to a still unknown destination. We have heard the unique voice of our calling, and begun to get in touch with our personal 'vocation' – something of the real direction and shape of our own role in the lived ministry of the Lord.

Before we move on, let us stop for a few moments to reflect on what we need to take with us. The Gospels give us all the clues we need. A few of them are listed here – perhaps the most important things. You might like to think about this 'packing list', that Jesus himself suggests to us. How do you feel about the individual items on the list? Do you have an adequate supply, and if not, can you ask the Lord to give you what you need? Is there anything you would like to add?

Prayer – the staple food and the essential living water of your journey. To make the Kingdom journey, to become and remain disciples of the Lord, we need to be in constant communion with him in prayer. In practical terms this means setting aside real time to be still in his presence, daily if at all possible, and to listen to the movements of our own hearts, where he is indwelling. There are as many ways of praying as there are pilgrims on the Kingdom road. If you would welcome some help in exploring some of these many ways, you might find it in the companion book *Taste and See*.

Listen to Jesus' guidance on prayer in Matthew 6:5-15. Ask him, perhaps, to take you to the Father and to hold you in his love as, together, you and he say the prayer that he himself has taught us. You might like to make this a part of your daily prayer. Share something of your prayer on a regular basis, if you feel able to do so, with a trusted 'soul friend' or with a small group of journey companions, remembering Jesus' promise given in Matthew 18:19-20.

Trust – the only quality that will keep you going, and growing. As you listen to Jesus' guidance on the importance of trust, notice how trust seems to grow out of a base-line of helplessness, not at all from our achievements. Being in touch with our own helplessness is not a comfortable experience, but it is precisely there that we learn how to trust. Jesus directs our attention to the tiny details of creation – the flowers, the birds. They have no degrees, no career paths, no endowment policies, yet in every generation they come to the fullness of their own unique being, more surely than we do ourselves. They teach us how to trust the present moment, where God is continually weaving his Dream.

Sit for a while at Jesus' feet, and listen to his wisdom about the flowers of the field, in Matthew 6:25-34. Take time to notice how you feel about what he is telling you here. Respond to him by opening up your own true feelings about this kind of trust. Don't be afraid to throw all your human arguments at him, and to tell him how unrealistic he is, if that's how you feel. Your real feelings are the starting point of every new growth spurt.

Integrity – the willingness simply to be true to yourself. There is no room for false positions or pretensions on this Kingdom journey, which we all share in radical equality. What is sound in us will bear good fruit, and what is unsound, the Lord will strip away, in his own time and his own way. We are walking together as companions, not as members of an army platoon bound under obedience to any fallible human authority. The journey asks us to respect the authority of the Lord within our own hearts and within each other's hearts. This is the only authority we can trust.

Trust begins with
helplessness and grows
us into who we really are

Listen to what the Lord has to say about the foundation stone of integrity, in Luke 6:39-49. The one who learns, he says, is not superior to the one who teaches, but the one who learns well, from a sound foundation, will also have something to teach. You might like to reflect on how you feel about the foundation of your own life, and whether it feels like rock or sand.

Readiness – to expect the unexpected, because the action of God in our lives will constantly take us by surprise. Readiness doesn't mean a succession of all-night vigils that leave us drained and exhausted, but a refreshed and wakeful awareness, to notice every sign of God's presence in our world and our daily living.

Read the parable of the ten bridesmaids, in Matthew 25:1-13. Try to let the action come alive for you in your own situation. I once had the privilege of hearing a lady from Liverpool relating this story in her own way and her own language. She built up the tension as the day went on and the bridesmaids (small girls in her story) moved from excitement, to fractiousness to thorough-going bloody-mindedness, until the cry went up: 'Here he comes – I can see him – he's coming down the East Lancs Road!' Tell yourself this story in your own way, and let the Lord come to you along *your* 'East Lancs Road'.

Wholeheartedness – the antidote for the inevitable weariness and self-doubt that afflicts the serious traveller from time to time. As we gather at his feet, to learn from him how to make this journey, Jesus continues to remind us that it will not be a bed of roses, and that we will sometimes be tempted to turn back. How do we retain the wholehearted enthusiasm with which we first set out? You may have your own remedies. One such remedy might be the supporting companionship of other pilgrims who will carry us when we are too tired to walk. Another will certainly be to return, in prayer, to those moments when we knew the felt presence of the Lord in our lives and heard the voice of his calling.

Listen to Jesus' words in Luke 9:57-62, and again in Luke 14:34-5. He doesn't ask us never to feel weary, but to encourage each other in our weariness. He reminds us that our deepest desire is to be with him, on the journey, and that our joy can be found only in moving forward. How do you feel about what you read here? How do you want to respond? Let your response come from your true feelings, not from what you think you 'ought' to feel. What helps you, personally, to keep going when your enthusiasm is flagging? How can you encourage others?

Discernment – the compass by which we find our way. A discerning heart is one that can distinguish between what is leading us closer to God and furthering the coming of his Kingdom, and what is leading us away from God, and impeding the coming of the Kingdom. It is the ability to recognise what leads to Life, and what tends to be life-destroying and to act on what we find. The growth of discernment is the task of a lifetime. What is life-denying can come in many disguises of 'good', and what is life-giving may at first seem fraught with pain. But discernment grows sharper every time we exercise it, and we exercise it most effectively in prayer, and especially in the prayer of reflecting back over the events and movements of each day (see Chapter 2).

Listen to the warning of Jesus in Matthew 7:15-29. Take seriously the dangers he talks about, but hear, too, his promise of the gift of discernment. Notice the infallible test he gives us, to use as we journey: '*By their fruits you shall know them*'. If something in our lives bears life-giving fruit, for ourselves and others, then we can be sure that it is of God.

Detachment – the ability to avoid getting sidetracked. Especially today, in a consumer society that values comfort, status and satisfaction of every kind so highly, we walk a continuous tightrope, trying to find a balance between genuine material needs and the kind of radical emptiness in which Jesus lived his earthly life. Jesus seems to teach us that it is not things (or people) in themselves that are harmful, but our *dependence* on them. As long as we are in a state of dependence on all that we think we can't live without, we will not be free to journey on. Like discernment, the practice of detachment is a life task, and one that we will never fully complete. If you would like to explore its implications more fully, you might find the companion book *Landmarks* helpful.

Listen to Jesus' wisdom about the difference between material and spiritual treasure, in Matthew 6:19-21. Take some time to reflect on what you most treasure in your own circumstances. If your home burns down tonight, what single thing would you most want to rescue? What does this tell you about the direction of your own desiring? What quality or aspect of your life do you most dread losing? Tell the Lord about your deepest fears, without holding anything back.

We have gathered round the Lord, as fellow pilgrims and apprentice disciples, to listen to his guidance on what to take with us on the Kingdom journey. The things we have looked at in this 'packing list' won't take up any room in our rucksacks. They won't incur any excess baggage charges at the airport check-in. Jesus looks round at us now, with a loving smile, and tells us that all we really need is 'nothing'. 'Take nothing for the journey,' he says. 'No bread, no haversack, no travellers' cheques. No spare clothes. Wherever you are welcomed, stay there. Wherever you are rejected, move on' (Mark 6:7-13). But notice, too, that 'he sent them out in pairs' (v. 7). Don't go without your 'soul friend(s)'. Don't make the journey without Christian companionship.

Everything but the truth

Our apprentice journey, as I imagine it, is a mixture of times spent together, learning from the Lord, hearing his wisdom, his instruction, listening to his stories, watching him in action, and times spent apart with him, alone in prayer, reflecting in our own hearts on all that he is teaching us, and allowing him to open us up to an intimate friendship with him.

Before we move on, let us just pause for a few moments now to think about the nature of those 'times apart', and just how open and honest we feel we can be in the way we approach God in prayer and in our living.

I remember, with gratitude, the wisdom of someone who once accompanied me during a retreat. I had spent the first couple of days reflecting on some Scripture passages he had suggested. I had been praying them imaginatively, and trying to make real connections with my lived experience. I felt that I wasn't doing too badly at all. Then he arrived in my room on the third morning, having obviously decided that I needed a kick-start.

'Margaret,' he told me, 'I want to introduce you to three different types of people in prayer. The first type of person recites set prayers and does spiritual exercises by the book.' No, I thought to myself (a touch self-righteously), that's not me. I've gone past that stage.

'The second type of person,' he went on, 'really prays from the heart, really enters deeply into the Scripture and experiences their own connection with it. They allow the Lord to open up his meanings for them, and they talk to him, friend to friend, listening to what he is saying to them.' I began to get a warm feeling. Yes, I thought. I can relate to that. 'But,' he left a pregnant pause, for the 'but' to sink in, before continuing, 'they pray about everything *except* the one burning issue in their lives – the one thing they don't want to look at.' There was silence. I recognised myself at once. My crest fell!

'The third type of person,' he concluded, ' is truly able to bring themselves, just as they are, into the Lord's presence, and be open to whatever comes up. They are willing to take off the censorship filters, and let God be God in their lives.'

I'm glad to say that the retreat moved on from there and bore fruit, but I am continually reminded that my temptation is always to slip comfortably into the 'second type of person' and keep God out of the very thing that needs him most. Only this morning, for example, having recently returned from two weeks away, where prayer had been erratic, I found my stillness continually disturbed by the memory of two particular people who have given me grief, and who keep on and on trying to force their way into my prayer. Just as insistently I keep cramming them out of it, pushing them aside as if they were distractions. In fact, of course, they represent the very issues I most need to pray about.

It is all too possible to offer God everything but the truth, when we approach him in prayer. The same is true of our daily living, and the choices we make along the way. We may even face such a situation in our choosing to follow the call of the King. Let's have a look at how our mythical 'three persons' might react to the call to make the Kingdom journey:

- The first type of would-be disciple looks at the conditions and wants to follow, but can't bring himself to give up the comforts and securities that he treasures – at least not yet. Make me good, Lord, but not today! He keeps on putting off the day of setting out, until eventually there are no days left, and he has missed his chance.

- The second type of would-be disciple reacts in the opposite way. She wants to say 'Yes' to the call, and in her determination to do this thing properly, she sells up her home, leaves her family with Grandma, quits her job and decides (for herself) that she will go to some distant part of the earth and 'save' it. Notice the one step missing from all of this – the humble question 'What do *you* want me to do, Lord?'

- A third type of would-be disciple would place themselves in God's hands, while retaining an alert watchfulness for any signs of where they might genuinely be being called. In this way God is given space to suggest his ways to our hearts, without being constantly blocked by our lethargy or pre-empted by our determination to do our own thing 'for him'.

The first two reactions represent an 'either-or' approach. Either I am committed and active for God, or I am not. If I am then I must make sure it shows.

The third reaction represents a balanced, 'both-and' approach. I am myself, with my own desires and fears, strengths and weaknesses, and God is God. I want to be at balance in this relationship, trusting that God will open up the ways he wants me to travel. Meanwhile I will attend to his presence constantly in my prayer, so that I may recognise every sign of his action in my life.

Only the third type of response is truly focused on God, just as only the third type of prayer was truly open to the movements of the Holy Spirit. We do well, at this point, to reflect on where we find ourselves among these types of reaction to God's calling.

Take a little time in prayer to reflect on these three ways of approaching prayer, and of responding to God's calling. Of course, they are oversimplifications, but they contain a kernel of truth that affects us all. Don't be despondent if you find yourself stuck in the 'second way' for most of the time. If we had already arrived at our destination, we wouldn't be making this journey.

Read and reflect on the story of the 'rich young man' in Mark 10:17-22.
Let yourself be present to the incident where Jesus calls this eager, enthusiastic young man to follow him and become a disciple. Notice the reactions in the young man, and in Jesus himself, when the young man hesitates, suddenly facing the cost of his discipleship. Like most of us, he is stuck in the 'second type' of reaction to Jesus' radical call, and still clinging to his own way of doing things. For him, the 'one thing necessary' would be a detachment from his dependence on his wealth. Let your own feelings open up in prayer, as you reflect on this incident. Is there anything in your life that God might be suggesting as the one thing you need to look at. Is there anything you may be avoiding, which is potentially a block to your following the Kingdom way? Whatever you discover in this prayer, don't fail to register the expression in Jesus' eyes as he 'looked steadily at him and was filled with love for him.' Let that look of love rest upon you, too.

Learning from creation

A little light relief now, after all the soul-searching. The apprentice journey continues. We might imagine a bright, sunlit day, and a group of disciples, ourselves included, walking easily alongside the Lord, stopping freely wherever there is something to notice. The purpose of our wandering is just to listen, and to let Jesus draw our attention to what we encounter along the way. His purpose is simple too: he wants to show us what the Kingdom of God is like.

We are still marvelling at all we learned a few minutes ago from the daisies and the sparrows in the field around us. Wisdom about living in the present moment, and living in total trust, and how much more freely we become who we really are, when we are not bent double with 'baggage'.

But now Jesus points to the field ahead of us. 'Look,' he says, 'there's a man sowing corn. See what happens to the seed.' Our own eyes, un-accustomed to seeing beneath the surface of things, are still focused on the distant figure of the sower, but Jesus can already see the mystery latent within every seed. 'Some of it will fall on the path,' he tells us, 'and be trampled. Some will blow into the stones, and never find any root. Some will stray into those thorn bushes and be choked. But some of it will fall into those rich, deep furrows, take root, grow and produce a hundred times its own weight in harvest. That's what the Kingdom of heaven is like. It's like a seed of something so life-giving that everyone longs for it, and everyone receives it. But some people's hearts are so choked with fretful-ness that the seed can't take root, and others are so dried up with care and worry that there is no soil for growth. For some people the Godseed in the core of their being is trampled to death by others. But many people have a heart that is open and receptive like those furrows over there. Their Godseed will grow and produce abundant fruit.' He leaves us to ponder this picture for a while. Then he goes on to talk to us about how the seed does its growing.

'You'll see,' he says, 'that once the seed has been sown, the whole process of growth happens on its own. The Godseed in your hearts is like that too. Once God has sown it, it will grow, without your doing anything. It will grow silently in the darkness within you, like a baby in the womb. You won't realise what is happening until, one day, the tiny new shoot of your heart's eternal life starts to show in your daily life. It will amaze you, that such a tender shoot has appeared apparently from nowhere, and how quickly it grows to ripeness, until it is ready to yield fruit for others.'

We pass a large spreading tree, growing close to the path. Again, Jesus stops and we gather round. He plucks a seed from it, and hands it round to us. The seed is so tiny we can barely see it, and everyone is afraid of dropping it. He smiles: 'Such a tiny seed,' he says, 'in fact it's the smallest of all the seeds, but just look at the great bush that has grown from it. Notice the birds nesting in its branches and see how much cool shade it casts. This is a measure of all that can – and will – grow in your own lives, from that tiny Godseed that the Father has sown deep within you.'

Read these parables for yourself, in Mark 4:1-9 (the sower), Mark 4:26-9 (the seed) and Mark 4:30-2 (the mustard seed). Take time, in prayer, to remember your 'Godseed'. Where do you feel there has been stony ground, rocks, or thorniness in your life? Where are the fruitful furrows? What about your relationships: which of them make you 'grow', and which of them deaden you? Are you happy with what you find? If not, can you do anything about it? What kind of 'soil' does your friend-ship offer to others? What about the growth of the Godseed within you? Have you noticed any shoots yet? Often we see the growth of God more easily in others than in ourselves. If you can, share with a friend the ways in which you notice the Godseed growing and sprouting in their lives, and let them do the same for you.

Eventually our walk brings us to a small cottage. Jesus is obviously a welcome guest here. The woman of the house invites him in and we follow. She is in the middle of a baking session. 'Look,' Jesus tells us. 'See the dough rising over there. The yeast is making it rise, though you can't see the yeast – it is completely mixed in with the flour and the water. The presence of God is like that. You can't see it or measure it, but it is in every-thing, giving life to everything. It is in you, making you alive, growing you, turning you into people who will give life and nourishment to others.'

We shake our heads. No, surely not us. We can never be people with anything to share with others. We're not gifted like that. But Jesus isn't having any of it. 'Is that how you really feel?' he asks. Then he points to the little brass lampstand on the cottage cupboard. 'Look at that lamp,' he says. 'She has put it on a shelf where it will give light to the whole house. But you would rather keep your God-given light hidden away under the bed? Just think about it.'

Evening is drawing in and the man of the house comes home. We see

A forest within every acorn ~
God's Kingdom
within every heart

at once that he is a shepherd. He sets his crook down and greets Jesus like a long-lost friend. It's been quite a day. He's been out on the hillsides searching high and low for one of his sheep that strayed. Now he has found it again, and rescued it from a hazardous cliff-face, and the relief and joy are written all over his face. Once again, Jesus seizes the opportunity to continue our education. 'That's what the Kingdom is like,' he tells us. 'God loves each of you so much that he will drop everything to come in search of you, should you stray. In fact,' he adds, almost under his breath, 'that's why I'm here with you now.'

Read these familiar parables again, in Matthew 13:33 (the yeast), Luke 11:33-6 (the lamp) and Luke 15:4-7 (the lost sheep). Let Jesus tell you these parables directly, and personally, and ask him to show you any ways in which they especially relate to your circumstances.

How do you feel about your relationship with God getting all mixed up, like the yeast, with your daily living and with the world around you, until it is impossible to separate them? How does it feel when you are asked to let your light shine? Would you feel safer keeping it under the bed? And do you remember any times when the 'shepherd' has come looking for you?

Night is falling, and we move on, to our night's encampment. (You will remember that 'foxes have holes and the birds have nests' but those who are disciples of the Lord must not expect a permanent home in the way the world expects it.) It has been a day of learning, and just when we think it is over, Jesus sets us our 'homework'.

In his parables, Jesus shows us, again and again, how the simple things of creation and of daily life can teach us the eternal truths about God and God's Kingdom. He uses pictures that are familiar to the people of his time and place.

Tomorrow, take the time to notice the little things that happen to you, or anything that catches your attention. Imagine that at the end of the day someone is going to ask you, 'What is the Kingdom of heaven actually like? Give us a clue.' Using pictures and examples from your personal, lived, experience – pictures that are familiar to people of our age and our culture – tell them in your own words: 'The Kingdom of heaven is something like this …'

Who are you, Lord?

The night is dark, the stars are bright, and the campfire is blazing. We are still buzzing with all we have learned during the day, and the same question is on all our lips: 'We can see something of what the Kingdom of heaven might be like, Lord, but who are *you*? How can we understand what you mean by "the Son of Man"? Tell us about yourself.'

A tall order? Indeed, whole libraries are filled with writings about what 'Jesus of Nazareth' is about, and Bibles are studded with copious footnotes to help us penetrate the impenetrable. Jesus himself has no such problems. He sits among us, at the simple supper table around which we are gathered beneath the night sky, and shows us, picture by picture, something of who he really is.

'How shall I begin to show you who I really am?' he murmurs. Then he stretches out his hand and takes a piece of bread from the basket on the table. 'Look at this piece of bread,' he says. 'You eat bread every day, to keep

Gathered around the fire of
God's presence,
telling our stories,
telling the God-Story

your bodies alive, but your trust in me, and in the Father who sent me, is what brings your true self, your deep, inner, eternal life to fullness. I am the bread that makes your Godseed grow.'

He passes the fruit bowl round, and we all help ourselves to dessert. 'Look at these grapes,' he urges us. 'They are another picture of who I am. The grapes are yourselves, full of life and flavour, each one unique, but all joined to the same source of life. And I am the vine on which each of you is growing. As long as you are on the vine, you are connected to everything you need to live and grow, but as soon as you are cut off, you can do nothing. If I am the vine, my Father is the vineyard keeper who looks after the vine, watering and weeding and pruning it when necessary, cutting away everything that might harm its growth. Remain in my love, just as these grapes have remained on the vine, until the time for harvest. Then I will remain in you, just as the life of the vine remains in every grape, holding it in being.'

The candlelight catches the Lord's face and lights it up in a moment of radiance, as we listen to him around the table. 'See the candle there,' he points to it. 'I am like the candle. My earthly life will burn down, just as yours will, but in my living I will give you all the light you need to find your way through all the ages that lie ahead. Stay close to me, in your living and in your prayer, and the world will never again be dark for you. You know yourselves that light will always banish darkness, but the darkness that is all around us now, this night, has no power to extinguish this candle. That is what I am like. A light shining for ever in the world's darkness, a light that can never be put out. And my light kindles yours, so that you too will be candles, your lives burning down to give light and warmth to a cold and darkened world.'

The stillness of the night is broken only by the Lord's words, and the distant bleating of the sheep on the fells. 'Listen,' he says. 'Hear the sheep bleating. They are crying because they are lost. I am like a shepherd, come to gather the lost sheep of creation and lead them home to the sheepfold. Not every shepherd means well. Many will put their own welfare before that of the sheep. But I am the good shepherd. I will die for love of the sheep I have come to gather.'

'But now you are tired,' he says, as he glances round at our faces. 'It's been a long day.' Yet, strangely, we don't feel tired. Our feet may be aching, but our hearts are light and we feel more fully alive than we have felt in ages. He smiles. 'I'm glad,' he says. 'Because you have discovered for your-selves that I am a gentle master. To walk with me, to learn from me, to become my disciples is not a burdensome journey, even though it may lead you through many hardships. The joy it generates in your hearts will make the path easy. The joy will far outweigh the pain you have to bear for my sake.'

Tomorrow the journey goes on. And through all our tomorrows. But there is no fear there. Sitting with the Lord, and listening to his Word feels like all we will ever need. He reads our thoughts: 'The journey is one of joy,' he says, 'and I am the Way on which you walk, the Truth that you are searching for, the Life that will make you fully who you are created to be. Now put your finger on your own pulse. Feel the throb of life pumping through your body. This is the outward sign of the power of your heart, generating life in you with every breath you take. I am like that pulse beat within you, vitalising you with the hidden energy of the Father, and closer to you than you are to yourselves.'

He tells us again, that he is with us always, even to the ends of the earth. And as we sit there, feeling our own pulses beating, we know, in a quite new way, how real and permanent that indwelling presence will be.

Read for yourself some of Jesus' self-descriptions. As you read the words, just allow them to soak into your mind and heart. Notice any word or phrase that stands out for you in a special way. When you find such a word of phrase, stay with it and ponder it. Carry it through the day with you, and keep returning to it. The fact that it leapt out for you means that your psyche is registering some connection with it. It has something to say to you. Chew on it, until you have extracted all the flavour from it.

Jesus, the bread of life	(John 6:34-40, 44-9)
Jesus, the true vine	(John 15:1-6)
Jesus, the light of the world	(John 8:12)
Jesus, the good shepherd	(John 10:1-18)
Jesus, the gentle Master	(Matthew 11: 28-30)
Jesus, the Way, the Truth and the Life	(John 14:6-7)

Choose a symbol or image or object from the familiar world around you to express what Jesus most means to *you*.

The mission statement

Every little business and every social club has its 'mission statement' today, so that the term has become seriously devalued. Nevertheless, as we embark on the Kingdom journey, we should take a moment to reflect on what our own 'mission' is about.

Jesus gives the clearest statement of the purpose of his mission in the synagogue in Capernaum, by quoting the prophet Isaiah, and affirming that he is himself fulfilling the prophet's vision, in his own living, in the here and now. He calls us to do no less!

The terms of the mission statement are unambiguously clear:

- to bring the good news to the afflicted,
- to set the captives free,
- to give sight to the blind,
- to lift the burdens from the oppressed,
- to proclaim God's love and forgiveness to all.

This is not just a mystical path of illumination and self-fulfilment that we are about to enter into, but a life of labouring for justice and for peace.

The mission statement is delivered in public – it begins in the Church, but clearly points the way beyond the boundaries of any institution. It is rooted in the history of the human search for God, and it transcends it. It is pure idealism, and it demands the most radical *real*-isation. It is hard to avoid the conclusion that if our churches today were living out this mission statement, we would be trampled in the rush of young people, fired by ideals and alive with creative energy.

So Jesus presents us, his fledgling disciples, with this burning statement of where we are going next. Then he turns our own question back to us. 'I have told you something of who I am. What about you? Who do you say that I am? What do I mean to you? Are you willing to be part of this mission?'

Read the 'mission statement', in Luke 4:16-24. Imagine Jesus delivering this speech in your own church or community. What does it mean to you? How do you want to react? The faithful of Capernaum reacted by driving Jesus out of town and trying to throw him off a cliff. Tell the Lord, in your prayer, about how you really feel. Show him any fears and doubts you have.

Now read Jesus' challenge, in Luke 9:18-21. He is asking you to move beyond mere knowledge to commitment, and beyond the authority of Scripture, to the authority of his living presence in your heart and your life. He is asking for your personal engagement with his mission. How do you want to respond?

Can we look into his eyes, in the light of all he has taught us so far, and say, with his first disciples: 'Lord, this is real. This is the most real thing there is, and I want to engage my life with yours, and with your mission for the world. You are the Christ, and my personal experience of knowing you and your love is the only solid ground I can truly trust, for the way ahead. Let me follow you and be part of all you are'?

7. LIVING PATHWAYS

For as long as I can remember, the sight of a freshly ploughed field has always fascinated me. As I write, the year is just turning from the brash brightness of summer to a subtler mellowness that heralds the coming of the autumn. The farmer arrived yesterday in the field that adjoins our garden, to do his annual ploughing. Every year it happens, and every year it takes me by surprise. Suddenly the familiar view of fading, jaded grass has changed overnight to the bare furrows of new-turned earth.

It was just such a sudden change of the landscape that Jesus must have brought about, as he walked the paths and fields of Galilee with his friends. All at once the terrain that had been so familiar, with its well-trodden paths and its centuries-old ways of doing things, was being upturned and reshaped. What had been hidden was brought to the surface, for all to see. The familiar paths disappeared among the new-turned furrows of a truth that caused the received certainties to topple. The rule of law was evolving into the reign of love. The old testament of promise was becoming the new testament of fulfilment. Yet so many of the signs of that growth and change appeared to be disturbing and even threatening – at least to those whose mindset was fixed on maintaining the status quo.

When I look at the field outside my window, I know that, for a while at least, those who used to walk across it will no longer be seen. For them the terrain has become non-viable. If they attempted their regular walk now, they would stumble among the deep ridges of earth. But I also see a flock of birds feasting on the wealth of new food that the plough has uncovered for them from depths they could never have dreamed of. A new population has sought out the field, irresistibly attracted by the hidden harvest that the sharp blades have yielded. Jesus too traversed the fields of the human heart with the blades of truth and love. The old inhabitants were stripped of their solid ground and challenged into reappraisal. And a new flock followed in the wake of the ploughman. A flock that had never

When fixed certainties
disappear, a whole new
world of possibility
is opened up

known the luxury of security, and for the first time feasted on a food that
satisfied their deepest longings. Meanwhile the ploughman continued with
the task at the heart of his mission: to prepare the soil for a new seeding.

And still he continues. Now, two thousand years later, it is *we* who must learn to walk in the new landscape of his Kingdom; we who must let go of the received certainties; we who are nourished by a food we could not have dared to dream of before the plough moved through our being; and it is in *our* hearts that the new seeding is being prepared. Through this part of our journey we will follow the plough, and learn from the ploughman more of what it will mean to live, and bear fruit, in this new, uncharted terrain.

His Way – our pathways

In Chapter 4 we reflected on the fact that Jesus of Nazareth walked only one small part of this earth in one small region, making contact with just a few people. In his earthly life and ministry Jesus lived out just one man's human situation, yet he brought to earth the potential to redeem *all* human situations. This potential is being fulfilled, life by life, in those who walk his Way through all the generations. His is the Way. We are his living pathways, each of us living out the realities of our own personal circumstances and situations. Together, we live out every possible human situation. The call is to let our own living of our own circumstances, our own walking of our personal pathway, become redemptive.

We might imagine all creation as a dense forest, overgrown with every kind of entanglement and dark with the threat of unseen danger and malice, but also bursting with life and potential. The coming of Jesus brought Light into the forest, once and for all, but ours is the task of carrying that light into the farthest corners of the forest. Jesus carved a Way through that forest, but ours is the task of walking that Way through our own life's circumstances, so that our personal pathways become aspects of his Way.

There is one unique track through the forest that only *your* life, lived in *your* personal circumstances, can clear for God's love and grace to flow freely in that part of the darkness. Your particular track, traced through your life events, your relationships, your unique mix of gifts and weaknesses and your ongoing choices and decisions – your track is becoming a channel of God's redeeming love, if you are willing to live it through him, with him and in him.

As we move on in our Kingdom journey now, we will reflect on how we can make this call real and incarnate in our own living.

The foothills of humility

The image of the new-turned earth is a reminder that the Latin word for earth (*humus*) is also the root of our word 'humility'. Humility is a quality that is very easy to misrepresent in negative, and even fatalistic images. Yet the search for genuine humility can lead us towards something of what it might mean to live our circumstances in ways that are redemptive for all creation. Perhaps there is a clue in the connection between the earth from which we draw life, and the humility of spirit in which we approach the call to engage in the Kingdom venture. Both are about growing. And genuine humility of heart is the necessary precondition for such growth.

I saw the sunrise this morning. But not because I was in the 'right place' at the right time. At six thirty this morning I wasn't in the room that faces east, but in a room facing north. I didn't go to greet the sunrise, but the sunrise came to me. I became aware of a streak of warm light glowing among the branches of an oak tree in the neighbour's garden. It was this reflection that attracted me and drew me into the east-facing room to watch the miracle 'live'. This incident caused me to reflect on the many times in my life when I have not been in what I might have considered 'the right place', but how God has penetrated my being, indirectly perhaps, wherever I happened to be. It led me to think that perhaps every place is potentially 'the right place', and all that really matters is to be present to it at 'the right time'. And discovering 'the right time' is easy. The right time is always the present moment.

This little parable captures, for me, something of what it might mean to explore the foothills of humility. It speaks of simply being where I am and letting that place become a meeting ground with the ground of my being. This asks of me only that I *accept* the place I am (my particular circumstances of the moment, my gifts and weaknesses, and my existing relationships) with an attitude of openness – neither seeking credit nor assigning blame, without either complacency or resentment. Perhaps the beginnings of humility lie in this openness of attitude, this balance of response, to wherever we find ourselves, remembering that the north-facing window may reveal the sunrise as effectively as the summit of the mountain.

If we seek the wisest teachers of this art of being at rest in the here and now, with a heart attentive to the beyond, we need look no further than the basic elements of life.

One morning during a holiday with friends in the hills along the Polish–Czech border, I went for a solitary walk, and discovered a disused forester's watchtower deep in the heart of the woods. I climbed the ladder to the little wooden cabin at the top, and spent several hours up there, watching the trees all around, listening to the wind and the flow of the nearby stream. I found myself listening to the elements themselves, teaching me what 'humility' means.

- The water in the nearby brook told me how water always seeks the lowest point, yet has the power to dissolve the hardest rock, and to generate and sustain all life.
- The wind breathing through the branches all around me told me how the air is quite content to remain invisible, yet it is the breath of life, with the power to carry seeds across deserts.

Earth, water, wind and fire:
    teachers of elementary humility

- The fire, a constant threat in these summer-brittle forests, told me how fire is willing to serve us by bringing warmth to our winters and light to our darkness, yet to be consumed in the process.
- The ground below me told me how earth is content to be continually trodden on and walked over, yet it is the cradle of all our growth and the welcoming arms to receive our dying.

Creation itself seems to suggest that true humility has something to do with:

- accepting the circumstances in which we find ourselves, with a positive attitude
- actively seeking to bring life out of those circumstances.

In seeking to adopt a Christ-like *attitude* to the given-ness of things, we find ourselves already among the foothills of humility. Every time we choose to *respond* to particular issues in a life-giving way, we climb a little further into the 'holy mountain' of God's living presence in our world.

Called to grow

Jesus reminds us that he no longer calls us 'servants', but 'friends', because he is longing to reveal to us the deepest meanings of the reign of love (John 15:15). He is longing to journey with us beyond the limits of anything we can ask or imagine.

We begin our journey towards the fullness of our being by recognising that we are the creature, and God the creator. We, and all our circumstances, are part of God's creation. We seek to relate to those circumstances with the attitude that Jesus reveals in his own living. However unwelcome they may feel, they are the starting point of all our growing.

We move on to explore ways of being active channels for the coming of God's reign, within our own circumstances. We are no longer just creatures of God, but servants of God's Way. As the water sustains life, and the air carries the seed and the earth gives growth, so our living, the living out of our circumstances, can itself become a source of life.

As our experience of the True Life in Christ deepens, we begin to realise that what we desire above all is to be a part of God's reign and to be incorporated into God's Kingdom, along with all creation. We desire this so deeply that, if called to do so, we will *deliberately choose* even hardship and suffering, if this is the way to deepen our life in God. We are no longer servants, merely obedient to God's Word, but his beloved and intimate friends, ready to surrender everything to that friendship, as he has done for ours.

A Christ-like attitude – a personal engagement – a deliberate choosing. In this chapter we accompany Jesus further into his earthly ministry. In doing so we ask for:

- the gift of the first stage of this growth – to attune our own attitudes to his;
- the gift of the second stage – to recognise the ways in which we can use our circumstances creatively to become instruments of the coming of the Kingdom.

In Chapter 8, as we follow Jesus into his suffering and death, we move into the third stage of growth – the willingness to choose deliberately what may lead to suffering and hardship, if this is the way our desire to live the True Life should lead us.

Attitudes of Love

Our desire, as apprentice journeyers with the Lord, is to develop attitudes in our own living that reflect the Christ-like attitudes revealed in the gospel. In Jesus, God gives us a living pattern of the True Life into which he is calling us. Jesus continually reveals attitudes that are *life-giving*. They infuse love into every situation – sometimes a gentle, compassionate love, sometimes a tough and challenging love. He shows us how he embodied these underlying attitudes in the situations and circumstances of his own life. He calls us to develop our own Christ-like attitudes to the very different circumstances in which we live today in the twenty-first century. And he calls us to make our choices and shape our actions and relationships in line with these attitudes, so that our personal pathways may become aspects of his Way.

In this chapter we reflect on:

- Jesus' *attitudes* to the situations around him, noticing how he meets people and circumstances as they are and where they are, but also recognises the creative power latent within them;

- the ways in which Jesus *acts* in different situations, either to bring new life to them, or to change their direction from destructive to creative.

In the light of what these reflections reveal, we relate what we are learning from Jesus' model to our own circumstances:

- noticing our own underlying attitudes,
- allowing Jesus to redeem them,
- reflecting on how we are living out the True Life in our own circumstances,
- seeking to do so more creatively, by aligning ourselves more truly to Jesus' model, always looking for the more loving, more life-giving way forward in every situation.

And all the while we bear in mind the 'mission statement'. Jesus lives it out in every aspect of his own circumstances. He asks us to live it out in ours. He is the Way. We are the pathways reaching out in all directions from that Way – living pathways, opening up all of human experience to the passage of God's love and grace.

A phrase from a popular song caught my imagination recently: '*You are the words, I am the tune. Play me!*' This phrase summarises very well the call to become living pathways of Jesus' Way. Ours are the human cir-cumstances – all possible circumstances – that he comes to redeem and to fulfil. His is the life-giving, life-changing presence and energy that transforms those circumstances into the Kingdom of God. We, within our personal circumstances, are his living 'words'. He is the melody of Love. He calls us to 'play him', to make him seen and heard, felt, touched and tasted, in a world that is crying out for his Music.

We move on now to encounter the Lord in some of the places through which his Way leads.

Over the margins of acceptability

In a small neglected room a woman is struggling with her fears. For twelve years she has been suffering from menstrual problems that have meant virtually non-stop bleeding. She has tried everything, but no one has been able to help her. She is drained and feels tired all the time. Much worse, under Jewish law the bleeding makes her ritually unclean. So she is ostracised from normal society, forbidden to touch anyone because to do so would make that person likewise 'unclean'. She has been pushed over the edges of society through no fault of her own, and she has begun to believe that God must be punishing her for something, through this isolating and painful affliction. Suddenly she makes up her mind. If she can just touch the hem of Jesus' garment as he passes through, she is sure that she will be healed. And he will never notice her touch, in the throng and the tumult.

But Jesus does notice. He stops. He searches her out, and her terror at this dreadful exposure can be imagined. Instead of condemnation, however, she hears his words: 'My daughter. Your faith has made you well again. Go in peace, and in wholeness of body and soul.'

Men, of course, could also be 'unclean' in the eyes of society. Tax collectors, and anyone who colluded and collaborated with the hated Roman authorities, were prime candidates for social exclusion. We meet one of them at prayer in the Temple, alongside a righteous, law–abiding Pharisee. Listen to their two prayers, in Luke 18:9-14, and notice Jesus' reaction. The despised tax collector is well aware of his low ratings, and his self-esteem is equally low. All he can do is beg a loving God for mercy. The humble cry of his aching need reaches Jesus' ear. The self-satisfied attitude of the Pharisee brings his condemnation.

In a large Midlands town this week only one single Christian church was willing to welcome a group of gay Christians to celebrate a special service. How might Jesus have reacted: to the gay Christians themselves; to those Christians and their pastor who welcomed them; to those Christians and their pastors who refused their request?

Read the story of the woman with the haemorrhage in Mark 5:25-34, and of the tax collector at prayer in Luke 18:9-14. Which groups of people does *your* society most love to hate? Which groups tend to get pushed into invisibility: perhaps those with an unusual lifestyle or a different sexual orientation? Perhaps those who challenge our sense of justice and leave us feeling helpless, such as people of a different race, refugees, the elderly, the handicapped? Perhaps those with a criminal record, or those whom it is easy to use as scapegoats?

How does your faith community react to: AIDS sufferers, gay relationships, single parents, asylum seekers, ex-prisoners, crying babies, teenage music groups, jeans and tee-shirts, other denominations, honest discussions about controversial topics?

Imagine Jesus coming to settle in your town, renting a house in your neighbourhood, dropping in on your church. How do you think he would relate to these people? Talk to him about how you feel, and listen to anything he might suggest about how you could influence or challenge social attitudes in the way that he did.

Through the wilderness of sin

It's daybreak in the Temple, and Jesus is sitting quietly, teaching those who have come to hear him. The calm reflectiveness is suddenly interrupted by shouting and screaming outside the Temple door. A group of the religious leaders burst in, dragging a half-naked woman along with them. Triumphantly they force her to stand in front of Jesus. They have caught her in the act of adultery, they tell him, a capital offence for which she should be stoned. Imagine the clamour. Get in touch with some of the high emotion: the lust for revenge, the self-righteous indignation, the shame, the bewilderment, the terror. And the gloating question to Jesus: 'What have you got to say about *that*?'

Into the heart of all of this, Jesus moves with quiet wisdom and with compassionate love. He brings the scene to a point of stillness, and begins to write in the sand on the floor, with a stick. Eventually he breaks the silence. 'Let the one among you who is guiltless throw the first stone,' he says, and continues his enigmatic writing. One by one the accusers disappear. The woman is left alone with Jesus. 'Has anyone condemned you?' he asks her. 'No!' she says. 'Neither do I,' he responds. 'Go now, and break the sinful habits that held you captive.'

Evening now, and Jesus is enjoying dinner with a group of the Temple leaders. And once again there is an unscheduled interruption. A woman breaks in on the scene, determined to see Jesus. Everyone there knows what a bad reputation she has. A woman of the streets. Not at all the person you would expect to burst in on a gathering of those who see themselves as the pillars of society. We might allow ourselves the indulgence of imagining our own particular group of 'good and proper' folk whose dinner party is gate-crashed by someone who embodies everything they most despise.

Jesus resists all the pressure – spoken and unspoken – to have her removed. Instead he pays her real and loving attention, and lets her kiss his feet and anoint him with her ointment. As the scent of the oh-so-inappropriate perfume pervades this masculine gathering Jesus tells them a story. 'Imagine two people in debt,' he invites them. 'One owes the milkman for two weeks' deliveries. The other has defaulted on his mortgage repayments, had his house repossessed and is out on the streets. By a miracle, both debts are cancelled. Which of them will show the more love to the one who has paid off the debt, do you imagine?' 'The one who has had the larger debt cancelled,' they admit, with some reluctance, surely guessing that Jesus is leading them where they would rather not go. 'Exactly,' says the Lord. 'This woman here has had her many sins forgiven, and she knows the extent of the miracle of love that she has experienced. Her response of grateful love overflows all over me, in her perfume and her tears. But where is yours? All I receive from you is courteous conversation.'

Read the story of the woman caught in adultery in John 8:2-11, and the story of the interrupted party in Luke 7:36-50. Does anything in either of these stories make you feel uncomfortable? If so, don't judge yourself, but allow yourself, in prayer to be with Jesus in that particular place and ask him to open up the real roots of your feelings and touch them with his love.

Notice how Jesus turns an *attitude* of compassion into life-changing *action*. Are there any areas of your own experience that feel stuck between warm feeling and constructive action? Do you feel able to ask the Lord to lead you beyond felt compassion to practical action?

What people, or circumstances, bring out your inner critic most readily? Who are the people you try to avoid? Those of whom you would have to say: 'Anyone but them, Lord!' Imagine yourself invited by Jesus to a party with some of the people of whom you most strongly disapprove. How is the atmosphere? What difference does Jesus' presence make? Talk to him in your prayer. Tell him how you really feel, and let him respond.

And what kind of comments does your 'inner critic' direct towards *you*? Do they tend to stifle your enthusiasm and undermine your confidence, either directly or indirectly? Is this how you want things to be? Talk to the Lord about whatever you find.

In the jungles of injustice

If we are still tempted to imagine Jesus in the pictures of our childhood storybooks as 'gentle, meek and mild', a visit to the Temple might open our eyes to a very different aspect of his love.

Jesus and his disciples are making the journey from Bethany to nearby Jerusalem. The day, it seems, gets off to a bad start, when Jesus looks for some fruit on a leafy fig tree. Failing to find any he curses the fig tree, even though, we hear, it was not yet the fruiting season. This incident seems hard to understand, and perhaps it set the tone for the day, because we read that when the friends arrived in Jerusalem, Jesus went into the Temple and overturned the tables of those who had established themselves there as salesmen and money-changers. 'This is a house of prayer,' he cries. 'How dare you turn it into a place for making money, and exploiting people?' Those in authority in the Temple don't like this at all, and, we hear, start to look for ways of getting rid of this challenging truth-teller.

Was it just a bad day? Or was it the day that Jesus' anger and frustration spilled over, when he realised that the religious leaders of his day were obscuring the true purpose of his Father's Kingdom, and encouraging the agents of profit and exploitation in their midst? Was it perhaps also an expression of fury that the very people who should be serving and tending the coming-to-fruitfulness of his Father's people were actually blocking that fruitfulness – preventing the tree from bearing figs?

Read about these expressions of Jesus' anger in Mark 11:12-19 and in Matthew 23. Get in touch with the feelings of frustration and anger being expressed. Where do you find yourself in these incidents? What feelings do they bring up in you? What prevents the 'fig trees' of our own day becoming ripe and bearing fruit for all people? If you find any structures of injustice on your doorstep, is there any way in which you feel drawn to express your opposition?

Jesus' friends are gradually getting the message that the Christ-like attitude is always one of forgiving love and mercy, to those who waver and fall and find themselves in the captivity of sin. But those who would hold others captive through narrowness, bigotry, or the abuse of power must be rigorously opposed. The demands of mercy and the demands of justice are two sides of the same coin. Jesus speaks of such a situation with his friend Peter one day. We might translate its details into a contemporary situation:

A man has been caught claiming unemployment benefits, while continuing to work in a lucrative business. The magistrate has been merciful and has let him go free with a warning. The man goes home and catches his son stealing some small change to go to the football match with his friends. He beats the small boy, and forbids him to go out with his friends for twelve months. Imagine Jesus in this scene and listen to his reactions.

Read the parable of the unforgiving debtor in Matthew 18:21-35. Are there any situations you notice in the world around you in which you hear Jesus' challenge to forgive 'seventy times seven times'? Are there any situations that you feel would provoke his anger and his relentless call to justice?

Among the shadows of fear

The most frequently repeated phrase of Jesus is 'Do not be afraid!' Fear is one of the worst enemies of the Kingdom journey. It has the power to derail us from one moment to the next. How does Jesus face fear? We might spend a little time with two stories: one reveals Jesus' attitude towards fear in others, and one shows him facing a frightening encounter himself.

In one of the best-known Gospel stories we find Jesus' friends struggling to cross the Sea of Galilee in the midst of a storm, while Jesus himself sleeps peacefully in the stern of the boat. As the storm force increases, so the fear of the friends spirals out of control. Panicking, they wake him, quite unable to understand his apparent lack of concern. And he in turn rebukes the storm and restores calm, both to the elements and to the raging fears of his friends.

It is surprising how often, when people enter imaginatively into this scene in their prayer, they find themselves struggling with the storms of their own lives without ever thinking of 'waking Jesus up'. This incident challenges us to remember the promised presence of the Lord in the midst of our worst experiences, even though we may find it difficult to believe in that presence. Will we go with the fears? Or will we seek that deeper level of security in the ground of our being, the stern of our 'boat', where the Lord of peace dwells?

On the far side of the lake lies the territory of the Gerasenes, where another terrifying encounter awaits them. They are greeted by a man who is dangerously insane, and who roves the tombs, howling and gashing himself with stones. No chains can restrain him, so great is the strength of the destructive force within him. Jesus confronts this situation, and challenges the man to confront it in himself. 'What is your name?' he asks. 'My name is Legion,' replies the man, 'because there are many of us.' We might allow the Jesus revealed in this incident to approach us in our own worst fears, and ask us too, 'What is your name? What is your true self about?' And we too may have to reply, 'My name is Legion, because my true self seems to be all over the place, and I can't get myself together, whatever I do.' Jesus heals the demoniac by recalling him to his true centre, and reducing the many fears into their separate and manageable units, which can be conquered singly in a way that was impossible when they joined forces.

This story reminds me of one of my own experiences of sudden fear. I was walking along a main shopping street in a large town, with a friend. The street was busy, but peaceful. It was a Saturday afternoon. Suddenly the street was engulfed by a swarming mob of several hundred football fans. Collectively they were like an advancing army, trampling everything and everyone who got in their way. For a few minutes we were in real danger. We stepped back rapidly into a shop entrance as they surged past. Then I noticed an elderly lady confront one of them. She forced him to stop in his tracks, and he became separated from the mob. He was shaking, and for a moment I thought he was going to cry. He was reduced to the stature of a frightened child by her challenge. Singly, I realised, these young men were completely harmless. Collectively they were terrifying. My fears, I find, can be very much like that.

Read the stories of the calming of the storm, and the healing of the demoniac, in Mark 4:35-41 and Mark 5:1-20. What is the most frightening part of your life right now? Have you thought of 'waking Jesus up' and asking him to help you deal with it? Is there a particular person who is making you afraid? Talk to Jesus about the fear-ridden relationship. Ask him to show you the strength of his own power – the power of love – compared to the force of your fears.

In your prayer, travel with Jesus to the land of the Gerasenes. Where do you find yourself in this story? As you look into your own heart, can you see any evidence of the 'legion', the fragmentation and 'all over the place' feelings? The fear of being swamped by a thousand conflicting demands? Suppressed anger and resentments that continually try to break the chains of your self-control? Silent screaming in the face of all that seems to pursue you? Let Jesus approach you in your fears, and ask you calmly: 'Who are you? Where is your real centre?' Let him look into your eyes and see the fears raging inside you. Then let him take them one by one, face them honestly, cut them down to size and show you how powerless they are in the face of his protective love.

Along the corridors of pain

Wherever Jesus went, he found himself surrounded by throngs of people begging him to heal them, to make them 'whole' again and release them from every kind of brokenness.

One of the most striking features of the people who seek Jesus' healing is their *persistence*. One such patient was literally dropped through a hole in the roof by his friends in their determination to claim Jesus' attention. Another had waited for thirty-eight years at the pool of Bethesda in the hope of a miracle.

Read the stories of the healing of the paralytic in Luke 5:17-26, and of the man at the pool of Bethesda, in John 5:1-9. Reflect on the power of persistence, and patience, as well as the feelings of helplessness and trust, that these incidents reveal. Notice how Jesus reacts to the people involved, what he values and affirms in them. Reflect on any situations in your own life where there are feelings of helplessness, hopelessness, or simple 'hanging on in there'. In your prayer invite Jesus to come into those situations and touch them with his love. Does your prayer suggest any ways in which you might be a carrier of his healing and encouragement to those concerned?

Sometimes there can be subtle forms of pay-back in remaining unhealed. Wholeness, wellness, fitness can bring new challenges and disrupt our old coping mechanisms. Listen to Jesus' searching question to the sick man of Bethesda: *'Do you want to be well again?'* and reflect deeply on what your own answer might be. Be alongside the paralytic and his friends and notice how a desire for healing is answered by the granting of forgiveness. What does 'wholeness' mean to you? In what aspects of your living do you feel the need to ask for this 'wholeness'? Bring your feelings and desires to God in your prayer.

The 'mission statement' speaks specifically of 'giving sight to the blind', and we hear, over and over, of how Jesus gives not just sight, but *insight*, to those who are open to receive it. There are many kinds of inner blindness: blindness we inherit from our circumstances and from the prejudices around us; blindness to the things we dare not look at; the blindness of being lost in a tangle of experience in which we can no longer distinguish the wood from the trees.

The blind beggar, Bartimaeus, uses all his begging skills to attract Jesus' attention. **Read about his miraculous healing in Mark 10:46-52**, and reflect on where you find yourself in the scene. Listen to Jesus' question: 'What one thing do you most want me to do for you right now?' and respond to him. Can you remember any situations in which you might say that the scales fell off your eyes and you could see things in a different light? If so, take a moment to express your thanks. How has your life moved on since then, in the light of such new insight? Are there any areas where you feel you are still groping blindly? Can you talk about them with Jesus?

Not only our bodies and minds, but also our relationships and our sense of self-worth can be sick and broken. Jesus never fails to take the evidence of breakdown and despair deeply seriously, as, for example, during a journey through Samaria. Stopping to rest at a well, he encounters a woman there in whom he recognises the signs of a despair lightly disguised by a breezy and apparently confident exterior. He engages her in conversation, and uncovers a whole string of broken relationships in her story, and a well of unhappiness in her heart.

Read about this meeting in John 4:1-30. Get in touch with all the feelings being expressed here, and notice Jesus' attitude towards the woman, and the non-judgemental acceptance with which he listens to her story. If you feel able to do so, tell him your own story, and let his listening presence be a source of healing. How do you feel when he offers to give you 'living water', springing up from a well in your own heart that you may feel had long ago dried up?

One of the worst kinds of pain we encounter in our lives is that caused by rejection in its many forms – ranging from lukewarm indifference to outright antagonism. The mission statement calls upon us to 'set the captives free'. Can we really hope to be set free from our dependency on the good opinion of others, and the darkness into which rejection pitches us? Can we be liberators of others thus imprisoned? Jesus warns us of the inevitability of rejection in his story of the party that no one wanted to come to.

Read this story, in Luke 14:15-24. Imagine yourself in this kind of situation. Perhaps you have made a big effort to prepare something special for your friends or family, but the response is one of apathy. Lame excuses are offered. The truth is that your kindness is being rejected. You have given your best, and your best wasn't good enough. How do you feel? As you ponder this passage, just become aware of how Jesus handles it. Does anything you notice help you to deal with rejection yourself? What does the story suggest to us about the inclusiveness of our faith communities, our social groups or our families?

In the joy of friendship

Jesus valued personal friendship very highly. Let's join him on a visit to friends who frequently offered him a 'bolt-hole' where he could find shelter and peace amid the demands of his ministry. The scene appears to be peacefully domestic. One of the sisters, Martha, is working in the kitchen, busily preparing a meal. The other sister, Mary, is sitting with Jesus, just listening to all he has to say. Both are offering hospitality in the way they know best. But underneath the surface hidden resentments are brewing. Eventually Martha can't contain her frustration any longer: 'Am I to do all the work on my own? Tell Mary to come and give me a hand, Lord.' Jesus listens to the complaints, but then, surprisingly perhaps, defends Mary's choice. 'She has chosen wisely. What really matters is to be together and share what is in our hearts. Let's not be so busy that we miss each other completely.'

Read the story of Martha and Mary, in Luke 10:38-42. Do you have a 'bolt-hole' – perhaps special friends who give you space to be yourself? If so, remember them in prayer with gratitude. Does your friendship offer this kind of safe space to others?

Does your experience of friendship include permission to challenge, and be challenged, when this would be helpful to the growth of all concerned? How do you handle challenge? How do you react to it when you are on the receiving end?

Many of us will find both a 'Martha' and a 'Mary' within ourselves. There is a tendency to get carried away in fretfulness, and there is also a deep need for stillness and reflective conversation. We attend to our friends by actively serving their needs, and by simply relaxing in their presence. How do you feel about the balance of 'Martha' and 'Mary' in your own friendships?

Then again, sometimes Jesus' hospitality was on a much vaster scale. And clearly he expects his friends to extend friendship to all creation.

Read the story of how he produced food enough for thousands of people who had followed him out into the countryside, in Matthew 14:13-21. Notice the instruction: 'Don't send them away. Feed them from your own resources.'

How does this instruction speak to *you*? This miracle encourages us not to be deterred by the obvious inadequacy of our own resources, because the Kingdom operates a multiplication factor way beyond our imagination.

We began this chapter in 'the foothills of humility'. Before we move on, however, we might take a moment to enjoy the view from the mountain-top. Occasionally there are moments when the radiance of God's love

Moments of transfiguration
bathe our lives' landscape
in a different light

seems to break through our everyday experience, and flood the core of our being. Jesus allows three of his closest friends to share such a moment with him. Let God take you back to moments when your life has been momentarily transfigured, and you have known the reality of God in ways that no one can ever deny or denigrate. These are moments 'out of time' that we can never hold on to, yet can never lose.

A friend once described her experience of the joy of God's friendship as being like sinking deeper and deeper into an ocean, and then momentarily touching the ocean bed. We may lose that 'touch' almost immediately, and come back to our everyday concerns, but the fact that our feet have once touched the bedrock means that the reality of that bedrock can never again be doubted. What we have known, we know eternally, and we know it with a heart-knowledge that will outlive the eventual breakdown of our bodies, our minds, and everything we call our earthly life.

Read about Jesus' transfiguration in Matthew 17:1-13. This is a moment out of time and beyond place. Relive any timeless moments of your own, and connect again to the experience of God's presence that you knew then. Let the joy of that heart-knowledge give you new energy for all that lies ahead. Can you share anything of your own experience of God with your close friends, as Jesus did on the mountain of transfiguration?

Through the growing pains

The Kingdom journey will always lead us beyond today's horizon. As long as we live, we grow. Jesus shows us how to grow, when he allows us to share in some of his own growth points. One such growth point happens when he is travelling in the Gentile region of Tyre, and is asked by one of the local people to heal her daughter. At first he resists the request, pointing out that he has come for the lost children of Israel, and not for foreigners, and uses the example of a family meal, at which the children of the family, and not the household dogs, must be given the food. The woman is not to be easily put off, however, and reminds him that even the dogs are allowed to pick up the scraps that the children drop. Something seems to change in Jesus at this moment. He recognises the woman's faith, and the truth of what she is telling him. He heals the sick child, and moves on in his own

Kingdom journey with eyes opened in a new way to the claims of all God's people to the saving grace of the Good News.

This incident has a sequel. On his way back to Galilee from Tyre, the people bring Jesus a deaf man, also a Gentile, and ask for his healing. This time Jesus seems to show no hesitation. He touches the man's ears and tongue and prays simply: '*Ephphatha*' – Be opened! The man can hear and speak again. His world has opened up, under Jesus' touch, just as Jesus' own vision of his mission has been opened up, during this eventful journey through Gentile country.

Read these two stories in Mark 7:24-37. Imagine the 'children' of the family round the table, perhaps picking at their food, complaining about the bits they don't like and leaving half the meal on the plate. Now imagine the family pets waiting eagerly for any scraps that might fall in their direction, relishing them, hoping for more. In his hearers and his followers Jesus often found the attitude of the 'faddy children'. In the foreigners and aliens he often found an eagerness like that of the pets waiting under the table. What do you think he would find today if he visited our faith communities? Who are 'the children of Israel' for us, and who are the Gentiles? Now let Jesus share with you his own moment of growth and change of attitude.

If Jesus experienced growth like this in his own journeying, how much more must we be open to grow beyond our present assumptions? We might pray to 'be opened' to a way of living and loving from which nothing and no one is excluded.

Pathfinding?

We began this chapter by noticing what the blades of Christ's Truth and his Love do to the settled soil of our lives' fields, and we have accompanied him through a few of the most significant moments of his earthly ministry, noticing the constant calls to make connections with our own living and choosing. The Gospel stories are an inexhaustible goldmine from which we can harvest all we will ever need to know about what it means to have a Christ-like attitude to our circumstances, and to respond to whatever befalls us in a way that mirrors his Way.

How do we let our personal pathway become part of the Way? We might gather a few pointers from what we have been exploring:

- Identify the nature of your personal pathway. Get in touch with its shape and direction and terrain. What are your circumstances about? What gifts do you carry and what weaknesses are you aware of? What relationships form (or dominate?) your life? What events and choices are you facing right now?

- With all of this in mind, reflect on the statement: 'In *my* life, Christ is *redeeming* what it means to be . . . .' The possibilities are infinite: 'to be redundant', 'to be caring for a parent with Alzheimer's', 'to be in a failed relationship', and so on. Notice the italics in the statement. It is in *your* life (just as it is) that Christ is doing things, and what he is doing is *redeeming*.

- Ask continually: what would Jesus have done in this situation? Often the answer may not be obvious. If this is the case, modify the question: 'In this situation, which course of action (or which choice of words or response) is more loving and more likely to lead to life?'

The most effective way of discovering how Jesus himself would have reacted to different life situations is to steep ourselves in the story of his life, as revealed in the Gospels, and to try, as far as possible, to enter into these events with our *hearts*, as well as our minds

Check out regularly how your pathfinding is going, by using the daily review prayer suggested in Chapter 3 and by sharing your experience with other pilgrims who are also discovering their own pathways. And *check in* regularly with Jesus in prayer and conversation. It is he who sends us out with the promise: 'I am with you always.'

8. THE BROKEN GATEWAY

Walking our personal living pathways, through all the weather that life throws at us, sometimes calls us into the very place we would have done a great deal to avoid. I was reminded of this during a walk I once made in the Welsh hills.

It was autumn, and the weather was very unpredictable. The apparently bright afternoon was about to change into a threatening storm. I walked up the hill and reached the triangulation point at the summit. By this time a fierce wind was blowing, and I was finding it hard to stay upright. Instinctively I made for the shelter of the triangulation point and stood behind it, letting its bulk shield me from the gale force wind. But I soon realised my mistake. The wind howled past the triangulation stone and continued to blow me over. To be on the lea side of the stone was no help at all. I moved round to the other side, and leaned back onto the stone, facing the wind head on. And when I did so I found that I could stand there, quite safe and sure. The harder the wind blew, the more it blew me into the solid rock on which I was leaning.

The lesson was obvious. My faith was never intended to protect me from the many unwelcome things that life might throw at me. I could never find security by hiding *behind* the rock. My security was to be found in leaning *on* the rock and facing the storms in the certain knowledge that the strength of the rock would never fail me, and the worse the storm, the more I would become aware of the holding power of the rock.

Jesus demonstrates, again and again, the need to face life's situations directly, with an open and compassionate heart, and at the same time to lean back on the power of God who holds and sustains us. At this point in our journeying we come up against the choice of just how far we want to follow Jesus into the darkness – into the place of suffering and hardship where none of us – including Jesus – would, at a merely human level, have

The fiercer the storm, the firmer the rock

chosen to be. This is the point at which we are invited (not compelled!) to choose the deepest intimacy of a friendship that will trust the darkness – a friendship in which we desire to be with the friend, however destructive the circumstances, more than we desire our own safety and comfort.

Choosing for love

In the previous chapter we explored the first two stages of what it might mean to follow the Lord in authentic humility of spirit, first acknowledging wherever and whatever we are, without resentment or complacency, and then actively seeking to let those circumstances be life-giving, for ourselves and others. We looked at a very simple recipe for doing this – so easy to read on paper, so very hard to embody in our daily living:

> *In every situation choose what is more likely to lead to life.*
> *Choose the response that more truly reflects a Christ-like attitude.*

The recipe remains the same as we tread the boundaries of darkness in our lives and in our world. To choose to walk the ways that may lead to suffering, for the love of the friend we accompany, is to dare to step over these boundaries, with consequences that we cannot predict, trusting that the way continues to lead to life.

It is my privilege to know someone, whom I will call Jim, who dared to walk these boundaries in a way that seems very simple, yet for Jim was very costly. Jim's good friend, Jason, became clinically depressed. Jason seemed to sink, with terrifying speed, into a dark and bottomless pit. There was no getting through to him. He rejected every overture of friendship, and just wanted to hide himself away and lock the doors of his life against the world. He rejected Jim too, and Jim had real fears that Jason might take his own life.

Jim could have chosen to let Jason be, until the depression passed. Most people did just that. But, instead, Jim kept on visiting Jason, making human contact, simply 'hanging on in there'. It was probably the hardest thing he ever did. He didn't try to 'talk Jason out if it' or minimise the black pain that Jason was experiencing, or 'fix' the problem. He was just 'there'. His presence let Jason know that he wasn't alone in his Gethsemane. That was all. Months passed, punctuated by Jim's regular visits. Ever so gradually Jason began to show some response, as one emerging from an emotional coma. When the time was right Jim suggested a short walk along the road, then back to the safety of the bolt-hole. Then a little drive in the car. Then a trip to the shops. Before too long it was becoming possible to pick up the threads of normal life again. And after a year or more of Jim's patient 'being alongside' Jason returned to full emotional health. A Gethsemane experience had been passed through, and new life had been discovered on the far side of sorrow.

Crossing the threshold

When Jason became ill, Jim made a conscious decision to stay alongside his friend. He couldn't have known at the time what exactly that decision would entail, but he probably guessed that it would be costly in some way – not only in the demands on his free time, but also in the very real threat of being sucked down himself into Jason's negative and destructive feelings.

If we spool back now two thousand years we can observe another man about to cross an awesome boundary, for the sake of being alongside his friends in their need. Jesus is miles away, beyond the Jordan, when word comes that his dear friend Lazarus is dangerously ill. Lazarus' sisters implore Jesus to come to him. Yet, inexplicably, Jesus delays. He lingers for another two days before deciding to go back to Bethany. What is going on within him during those two crucial days? In Bethany he will restore Lazarus to life, and this act will certainly attract the attention of the authorities and hasten his own death. Lazarus' sisters, Mary and Martha, expect their friend, the healer, to be there for them in their need, and Jesus faces their reproaches when he arrives, apparently too late to save their brother. His own friends warn him of the obvious dangers of going back to the Bethany neighbourhood where the authorities are waiting to trap him. In this maelstrom of conflicting demands and emotions, Jesus makes the choice that is more likely to lead to Life – he decides to go to Lazarus and, in doing so, to make himself completely vulnerable to all that will surely follow. He follows what we might call the third stage of the way of humility, the pathway of extraordinary love, and deliberately chooses to cross the threshold of his own suffering and death.

Read the story of Lazarus in John 11:1-44. Try to imagine yourself present to one or more of the scenes described in it. Notice your own feelings and reactions. How do you find yourself responding? Do your responses connect to anything that is happening in your own life? Can you talk to Jesus about what you are feeling?

Is there something in yourself that is 'entombed'? Can you hear any signals in your heart urging you to 'Come out'? If so, listen closely to those deep desires. Could they be growing strong enough to overcome your fears?

Have there been any thresholds in your own life that you have felt you must cross, in order to be true to yourself, but that you knew would lead you into a place of conflict, hardship or pain? How did you react at the time? How might you want to react to similar situations in the future? Has anyone crossed a 'vulnerability threshold' of his or her own in order to be with *you* in a time of crisis?

There is something deep within us that recognises the power of living true to the core of our being, and having the courage to implement those 'true north' choices in our real day-to-day living, even when they bring us up against opposition and confrontation. Perhaps you have discovered, during these reflections, specific moments in your own life when you had the courage to 'live true', whatever the consequences. Perhaps you have recognised that courage in others.

The raising of Lazarus also raises Jesus' profile very significantly, and very dangerously, in the eyes of the religious authorities. Soon the time for Passover draws near, and there is a conspiratorial smell in the air. The wind is blowing up and human instinct is to seek shelter and keep one's head down. Jesus is once more with the family in Bethany, sharing a meal with the newly alive Lazarus and his sisters. Mary's understanding is dawning, about the cost of Jesus' love for them and for all of us. She responds by making a costly offering of her own, anointing Jesus with half a kilo of the most expensive perfumed ointment. Some silent voice in her is saying: 'I know that you are giving yourself totally, and I want to respond to you by giving myself totally to your great venture into Life.' Mary has crossed a threshold too. She has leapt over the boundary fence, to express her unconditional 'Yes!' to everything that the Kingdom journey will demand.

Read about this incident in John 12:1-11. Join Mary in that little room, where she has enjoyed Jesus' friendship all through the years. Use your senses to engage with the smell of death, seeping through every fissure, and the smell of overwhelming love and commitment, symbolised by the perfume. Recall any areas of your own life where the smell of fear or disappointment mingles with the smell of love and longing. Bring your feelings, your fears and your hopes, just as they are, to the Lord in your prayer. If you feel drawn to do so, let your heart speak its own 'Yes!' to the journey that now leads into an unknown darkness. You might like to express your feelings in some symbolic way.

To heaven alone, or through hell together?

I was praying one morning for two people who are very dear to me, both of them now dead. As far as I know, neither of them made any personal commitment to the way of Christ – indeed one declared himself to be an atheist all through his life (though I never quite believed him!). My prayer was simple, and one I commonly bring to God on their behalf. It amounted, more or less, to 'Please give them my love'. Then I found myself begging God to include them eternally in the circle of his love, whatever their limited notions of him might have been when they crossed the threshold of death. I found myself wondering whether I wanted, myself, to be included in a 'heaven' that *excluded* someone I love. I wanted to say: 'If you exclude them, Lord, you'll have to exclude me too.' Of course, words like that are easily uttered. Would we really surrender our hope of 'heaven', would we really walk a path that seems to lead to hell, for the sake of solidarity with those we love?

The memory of a Jewish friend's great uncle comes to mind: a medical doctor who miraculously survived captivity in an extermination camp, and, after liberation at the age of eighty-seven, simply returned to practise medicine in the devastated German community in whose name he had been despised and rejected. An unreasonable sacrifice – but he had a reason, the simplest and most compelling reason of all: 'The people need a doctor.'

Alice Thomas Ellis catches something of this imperative of all-inclusiveness in her book *The 27th Kingdom*: 'And yet, in the course of whatever passes for time in Heaven and Hell, all would be resolved, since the good deserve that the bad should be forgiven, the nature of goodness being to love'.

Perhaps this spirit expresses a little of what Jesus was living through in the week before his crucifixion. He has committed himself to us so totally that he can't go back to the Father without us. Our own commitment to those we love falls a long way short of this, but it helps us, perhaps, to penetrate a little way into the mind of Christ, as he deliberately chose the way that appeared to lead to the loss of everything, in order to bring us with him, home into the Father's heart.

We might let these thoughts shape our prayer as we stand with Jesus and his friends at the beginning of the final journey to Jerusalem – a journey from 'Hosanna!' to 'Crucify!'

Read the account of this last journey in Luke 19:28-38. Notice especially Jesus' instruction to his friends to 'find a tethered colt that no one has ever yet ridden' and untie it and bring it to him. The journey of love that leads to suffering is a journey that is personal to each of us – our own particular and unique 'living pathway'. No one has ever ridden the 'colt' that we must ride along this personal pathway to Calvary. No one can possibly predict how that 'colt' will behave, what the journey will mean for us, where and how it will end. We are asked to commit ourselves to the mercy of circumstances still to be revealed. Do you know anything, in your own life, of the nature of this 'colt' that you are perhaps already riding into an uncertain future?

For Jesus, the 'colt' soon proves dangerous, as the mood of the crowd shifts by one hundred and eighty degrees. Have you experienced anything of the jubilant affirmation, the adrenalin rush that lifts you above the crowds, and then its flip side, the undeserved and unforeseen change of mood, turning, perhaps, to jealousy, resentment, destructive hatred? If any experience in your own life reflects this kind of pattern, let it be the focus of your prayer today.

Is there anyone you don't want to 'go to heaven' without? If so, bring them into your prayer, and let your commitment to the ones you love flow into that total commitment of Jesus for all of us.

Committing . . .

The verb 'to commit' is a double-edged sword. If we give it an object, it usually means something bad, or even criminal. To commit a felony, to commit adultery, to commit murder. But if we let it be reflexive – that is, if we let it come back to focus on ourselves – it can express the highest and the best of which we are capable: to commit ourselves to a cause, to commit ourselves to each other, to commit ourselves to the Way of Christ.

Perhaps 'committing' is at the heart of what transpired at the last meal Jesus shared with his friends, the night before he was crucified. The world, as we can see now with hindsight, hangs poised between the worst and the best. In the hours that lie ahead, some will choose to commit treachery, violence, murder and suicide. Others will choose to commit *themselves*: to wait, to watch, to trust, and to follow.

Most of us will find something of ourselves in many, if not all, of these reactions. Our desire, in praying these events deep in the heart of our own being, is to recognise what we find there, and to bring ourselves and *all* our reactions into the healing presence of God. As we do this, we remember that this is the cutting edge of redemption. God is redeeming these very things within us, for our sake and the sake of all creation, and all he asks is that we open them up to him. The first essential, then, in entering this part of our journey, is honesty. What is there in *me*, of the appeaser, the betrayer, the denier, the deserter, and how do these things express themselves, concretely, in my living? What is there in *me* of the faithful companion, the one who serves, the one who waits, and trusts?

Let us, therefore, ask for the grace to acknowledge those aspects of ourselves that are tending to commit the worst, but also those aspects of ourselves that long to commit ourselves to the best.

And so we gather, Jesus' friends and companions, to share a meal with him that will prove to be the last. A Passover meal. And for us, too, a 'passing over', from the joyful, though challenging, intimacy of the journey through Jesus' earthly ministry, into the darkness, the fear, the threat of his dying.

The gathering begins with an unexpected, and perhaps slightly embarrassing gesture. Jesus rolls up his sleeves, wraps a makeshift apron round his waist, and bends down to wash our feet. Lovingly, gently, one by one he makes his way round the circle. For some of us this is the touch of love beyond imagination, as our feet – at once the most despised and the most sensitive parts of our body – are cleansed and soothed by the hands of one who loves us. For others it is simply too hard to handle. It reminds us of how far we fall short of being as loving to each other. And it requires us to expose to our friend our terrible need of cleansing – our thoroughly dirty feet!

This scene is still re-enacted ritually in some churches on the Thursday in Holy Week, and if you could do a survey of those Christians who take part in it, letting their parish priest wash their feet, I have no doubt at all that they would all admit that they had carefully washed their feet and changed their socks before they went to church that night. Jesus gives us no such option. He takes us off guard. His cleansing is for real – as real as our desperate need of it. And that is precisely the point. Redemption happens at the cutting edge – the edge where it is really needed – not in the areas that we have carefully sanitised beforehand. When we cover up our running sores with artificial piety, we do more to obstruct the flow of God's grace than when we openly rebel.

Read about this incident in John 13:1-20. Let yourself be present to the process, as Jesus goes round the circle. How do you feel when he reaches you? How do you want to react? What do you want to say, or do? Don't censor your reactions. Just let them be whatever they are, and let them reveal whatever the Lord is showing you through them.

Jesus says: 'I have given you an example, so that you may do the same for each other.' Think of the person, or group of people, whom you would most resent having to serve in this way. Take them into your prayer, and ask for the grace to find a way of expressing loving service, precisely for *them*.

Breaking ...

In these last days of Jesus' earthly life, everything is being turned on its head. This kind of loving confounds all our expectations. The raising of a friend back to life becomes the sentence of death for the one who brings life. The adulation of the crowds becomes a baying for blood. And now, gathered in intimate fellowship around the supper table, the breaking of a loaf of bread becomes the breaking of a life, and of all the hopes and longings that are pinned upon that life.

And just as we are called to model our service of each other on the example of the one who gently washes our feet, so this meal is also a call to 'do this, in remembrance of me.' As Christians we have spent the best part of two thousand years arguing over what Jesus actually meant when he handed round the broken bread with the words 'This is my body', and when he passed the cup round the table, with the words 'This is my blood'. Perhaps on this, our personal Kingdom journey, we might take a slightly different focus and reflect that *we* are the Body of Christ and the living river of his Life coursing through all human living. As he passes us the broken bread, he says to each of us: 'Be broken for each other. Pour yourselves out for each other. This is what it means to become my Body on earth.' He breaks us, for his world, and pours us out for each other, just as first he broke himself and poured himself out. But notice something else: before he breaks the bread at table, he *blesses* it. Whatever 'breaking' and 'pouring out' of ourselves may lie ahead along our personal pathway, it is enfolded in blessing.

Broken dreams and drained desires ~ the raw material of sacramental loving

If we can let this happen, we may discover that what we are actually engaged in is a different kind of 'breaking': a breaking of moulds or self-sufficient containers – the kind of breaking that opens up the husk of our being to expose the innermost kernel of humanity to the gospel of liberation.

Read the account of the Last Supper, in Matthew 26:17-35. Imagine yourself present at this gathering, and notice where you find yourself, and how you feel. Let Jesus pass the bread and the wine to you. Is there anything you want to express to him at this moment?

Bring to your prayer any memories you have of being 'broken' and 'poured out'. Perhaps you have looked forward to a quiet day getting on with something important to you, but one person after another has interrupted you. At the end of the day, the 'loaf' of your hopes for the day has been broken into many fragments, and given to those who asked you for your time and attention. Or perhaps the 'loaf' of your best years has been broken and given to your children, to a sick or difficult relative, to a demanding relationship or an exhausting kind of work? Has the 'wine' of your creative energy been poured out, unnoticed, so that others might grow into their own creativity? Has the 'cup' of your love been poured away into desert spaces where it seemed to bear no fruit? Listen again to the Lord's promise: 'When you have been broken and poured out for others, you have done this in remembrance of me.'

The breaking begins in the darkness of a quiet garden on the slopes of the Mount of Olives. Let us follow Jesus and his friends there now, to keep vigil . . . if we dare!

Deserter?

A TV documentary takes us back to February 1916. A shell-shocked soldier has been unjustly convicted of desertion by a hastily convened court-martial. Tomorrow morning he will be executed by firing squad. Tonight he sits alone in a makeshift cell, somewhere in France, while the rumble of battle goes on above his head. He hardly knows what is happening to him. He is stunned by the shell-burst that the verdict has detonated inside him. He writes a few lines to his mother. He thinks about God. He wonders. And his mind drifts into a black tunnel, darker than the darkness of the night.

The officers are relaxing over their food and wine. There is a false gaiety overlying the tension that the coming execution has generated. Fuses are short. There is an unspoken knowledge among them that something radically wrong is about to be carried out, but no one is responsible. All have the power of death. None has the power of life.

The chaplain leaves quietly and makes his way to the condemned man. His face is open and full of compassion. He asks if there is anything the soldier needs. The soldier stares in vacant disbelief at the question. What might he need, he wonders, if not his life? There seems to be no point in trying to reply. Dumbly, he hands the chaplain his last letter home, and the chaplain receives it respectfully. 'We could pray together,' he suggests. But the condemned man seems not to hear him. Their eyes meet for a moment, and a stream of mutual helplessness flows between them.

Perhaps the chaplain doesn't recognise God sitting there in the ruined man before him. Or perhaps he recognises him all too clearly, and the appalling truth overpowers him. He falls victim to his own kind of shell-shock. He turns. He deserts. Saying, as he goes: 'I'll be with you in the morning.' The prisoner stirs. Stares with wide, unbelieving eyes. 'In the morning?' he echoes. And the chaplain leaves, backing away from the black tunnel. Sympathy wasn't enough to get him through the night. Not enough to keep him with the helplessness. Authentic compassion might have served the situation better.

Read about Jesus' experience in Gethsemane, in Matthew 26:36-56, in the light of the story of the shell-shocked soldier. Where do you find yourself in the garden? Is there anything you want to say to the Lord? Have you met the 'soldier' or the 'chaplain' anywhere in your own experience?

The disintegrating shells

I have a little set of Russian Dolls – the sort that fit one inside the other. I have been amazed to discover that these dolls can 'talk'. They tell me all kinds of things about the Kingdom of God, and they have something to say about what happens when we surrender to the 'breaking' that begins with the Last Supper and the agony in the garden.

Imagine the scene. The Passover meal has been eaten, and the wine jugs have been drained. Who can tell what the mood of the gathering was like? Without doubt there was joy. Jesus says that he was longing to eat this meal with them (Luke 22:14-15), the last time they would share wine before they would rejoice together in an eternal reality. Surely, too, there was apprehension, in the face of the gathering storm clouds. This provocative, charismatic friend and leader had stirred up a hornets' nest. The hornets' wings were already whirring through the night air. And then there had been the strange incident with Judas. As if Jesus knew what was in the betrayer's heart, but allowed evil intention to take its inevitable course into destruction, and self-destruction.

The image of the Russian Dolls tells me a story about the agonising

*Layer after layer our false
securities disintegrate
until only the unbreakable
core of our being remains*

breaking of one layer after another of the 'securities' that seemed to
surround the circle of friends that night, and in which our own lives, too,
are cocooned. As we move more deeply into the darkness, we accompany

Jesus into the breaking of all those layers, acknowledging our part in this breaking, but also our sharing of the experience of being broken. Both these things are asked of us:

- To recognise at a very personal level what tendencies there are in ourselves, that lead us to betray, deny, abandon, compromise and destroy the True Life in the core of our being, and the True Life in each other. But to affirm and strengthen those tendencies in us to remain faithful, patient, and trusting, bringing the True Life to new birth in every generation.
- To expose, for healing, those parts of ourselves that have experienced what it feels like to be betrayed, deserted, accused and condemned.

We come into this experience both as perpetrators and victims, yet neither of these roles is the final word. The final word lies right at the centre of the set of dolls, and, as we shall discover, that centre is unbreakable.

The first of the outer shells to break apart after the friends' final meal together is the shell of trust. 'One of you who puts his hand into this basket of bread will betray me into death,' Jesus tells them, and everyone immediately protests his innocence. Yet Judas disappears into the darkness, to reappear in the garden, with an armed guard, to betray his friend, with a kiss.

We might imagine Jesus standing among us now, and challenging us like this: 'Today you worship me, and receive the bread and wine of my communion, but you are capable of betraying me and everything I am.' How might we react? Listen to the protests. But listen, as well, to the deep and painful truth. When the truth is acknowledged, the shell is broken. A deeper layer of honesty has been reached. The touch of redemption can penetrate more profoundly.

Jesus allows himself to be 'kissed to death'. 'Do it quickly, friend,' he speaks softly to Judas, reminding him, with these final words, that it is the sacred bond of friendship and trust that he breaks. And in the dark night, unseen, so many others are done to death under the guise of kindness. A bedroom door creaks open and a father enters the garden of his little girl, blasting her purity with his poisoned kisses. A mother beats her small son in a senseless rage, but insists on the goodnight kiss that preserves the seemliness of things. Children who tremble in the night, thinking only: 'Let it be over quickly.' As we think of these silent victims, we catch just one glimpse of what Jesus was absorbing into himself, when he accepted Judas' kiss.

Read the story of Jesus' arrest in Gethsemane in Matthew 26:47-56. Allow yourself to be present in the darkness, participating in these events. Notice whatever feelings arise in you – your response, for example, to the armed guard, to Judas, to Peter's drawing his sword, to Jesus' reaction, to the instinct of the disciples to flee from the scene. Be aware of your real and immediate response, before your mind gets a chance to rationalise it or 'clean it up'. If you can, talk with Jesus about your real feelings, whatever they are, and however unacceptable they may feel to you.

The outer shell of trust and the reliability of human friendship has been shattered. Jesus moves away, beyond the garden, to the time of trial.

The next shell to be broken is the shell of loyalty and fidelity. Over supper all the disciples have protested their undying love and faithfulness to their friend. Peter has gone so far as to declare that he is ready to go with Jesus to prison, and even into death. Indeed this will become truer than Peter can imagine, but Jesus knows that he is still very far from this degree of commitment. 'On the contrary, friend,' he warns him. 'Before this night is over you will have said three times that you don't even know me.'

When I read of this exchange I remember my own heartfelt promises made to God at my Confirmation, for example, and frequently in prayer, or to friends and family, in moments of extreme fervour. And I remember with shame, how I have failed to live true to these promises. How I have hedged about my faith, when surrounded by unbelievers. How I have been disloyal to those I love, when the going got tough. And I remember those whom I called my friends, who have stabbed me in the back, or simply gone off the boil and let me down when I needed them. I want to forgive. But I fail in that too.

Yet, ironically, Peter will indeed eventually follow his Lord to prison and to death. What heartens me in this incident is that Jesus is not condemning Peter for his failure today, but is accepting *today's* failure in the light of *tomorrow's* growth. A new, and stronger light beckons, beyond the dark tunnel of failure and fear.

Read about Peter's denial in Luke 22:31-2, 54-62. Bring to your prayer any memories of your own failures to live true to what is dearest to you. Let the hornets of reproach sting you, if they will, but then allow Jesus to touch the wounds – knowing you just as you are, and knowing that you are growing closer to the integrity you long for, through the depths of your failures and infidelities.

The Russian Dolls are getting thinner. The third shell to break is the layer of self-respect and dignity. Jesus faces mockery. He has moved, within a few short hours, from being surrounded by the warmth of friends he could laugh *with*, into the cold, threatening place where strangers are laughing *at* him, and trampling on the vision of love and peace and justice that he was born to embody. The respected leader has become the derided captive. The one who taught so many others the journey back to self-respect is stripped of all human dignity and diminished into the butt of course jokes. Something snaps in most of us if we feel we are being laughed at. He who laughs at us despises us. How do we feel about following him into this particular darkness?

Read about the ways in which Jesus is mocked, for example in Matthew 27:27-31, Luke 22:63-5, Luke 23:8-12 and John 19:23-4. Notice the feelings that rise up in you when you enter into these events. Allow your memory to reconnect to any times when you have made fun of someone, or diminished their self-esteem, and any times when this has been done to you. Talk to the Lord about your feelings, and ask him to let these feelings be taken up into the greater flow of his own patient loving.

Like most people I have had my share of scuffles with people over the years, and been accused of various wrong-doings – usually with justification – but on one or two memorable occasions I have known that I was being accused of something of which I was completely innocent. These incidents stand out in my memory to an extent far beyond the importance of the issue involved. I remember the anger I felt, followed rapidly by the helplessness of being unable to justify myself. My accusers were absolutely determined to have me 'condemned' and nothing I could have said could have deflected the charge, since they were operating their own agenda. At times like these it seems that our normal expectations of honour, integrity and justice completely break down, and the next shell of the dolls has broken up.

Jesus faces this kind of loss in his hearing before Pilate. Pilate embodies justice – indeed the full weight of imperial Roman justice and the freedom of the Roman citizen. Jesus, on the other hand, is accused of blasphemy and sedition, he keeps company with the most chaotic elements of society, he is a Jew, with none of the protection of Rome, and he is bound and chained. Yet as we watch this 'trial' unfold, we begin to realise that it is Jesus who is the embodiment of real justice, it is he who offers real peace, and it is he who is the truly free man, in spite of his chains. The false agenda comes face to face here with the True Life that it cannot tolerate. Pilate, the appeaser, tries to please all the different factions involved, including his wife, who has warned him to keep clear of this act of injustice. Jesus makes no attempt to appease, or to plead, or to justify. He allows the True Life to speak for itself. Eventually Pilate himself begins to see how truth stands firm and falsehood crumbles, but he lacks the courage to stand by what he sees. 'Truth,' he says. 'What *is* truth?' (John 18:38).

There is an appeaser in most of us at some level of our being, either personally, or collectively, in the way we allow our societies to function. The desire to please at all costs, can indeed cost us our integrity. We silence the cries from deep within: 'Be careful, you are not being true to yourself!' We try in vain, like Pilate, to wash the stain of collusion from our hands. We surrender our inner freedom, and often the freedom of others, for the sake of a quiet life.

Read about Jesus' confrontation with Pilate in Matthew 27:11-26, or John 18:28–19:22 (for a fuller account). Be present in your own way to the dialogue between the two men, and notice the interplay of false accusation and the silence, or the simple affirmation of Truth.

Do these events recall any memories from your own experience? If so, notice the feelings that are coming up in you, and talk with the Lord about them. Have you ever been wrongly accused? If so, how did you react at the time? How would you want to react if it were to happen again? Who are the people you habitually 'need to please'? Why do you think you react to them as you do? What power are you giving into their hands through your appeasement? What do your remembered experiences reveal to you about how you really want your life to be? Is there anything practical you can do, however small, to turn untruth back into truth in your own circumstances?

We are coming close to the innermost – and the most vulnerable – layer of our set of dolls. The cross is the place of ultimate loneliness, from which even most of Jesus' closest friends have fled. From the very bottom of this pit of despair he cries out to the Father, who also seems to have abandoned him. Perhaps it has to be so, that our 'dolls' have to be stripped right down to the innermost core, before the True Life is revealed. As this last layer of defence is peeled away, Jesus lets go of those he loves, and, finally, of life itself. The seed has to die, before the new life can germinate.

We have heard him tell us this so often, and our minds have digested it, but when we face the reality of it in our own lives, the pain is beyond belief. A browse through the newspaper will show us something of what this can look like here and now: a child is abducted, a beloved son is slaughtered in someone else's war, a cherished parent is swallowed up into the emptiness of dementia, a dear friend takes her own life. My God, my God, where are you in all of this, we might cry, and if we do we will hear our words echoing back to us from the cross, refusing to allow us to flee from the pain, because this is the very place that God is redeeming.

Read about Jesus' final moments, in Matthew 27:45-56. Bring to this prayer your own worst moments, your worst fears, your most destructive memories. Sit there, in your own Zero Hour, with the Lord in his. Scream your own 'Eli, eli, lama sabachthani' if you need to.

Night shift disciples

In a world of shadows a new darkness has fallen. The Light of the World, so it seems, has been permanently extinguished. Yet among those shadows there is a silent presence of those who long to follow, but are still ringed around by their fears. Night shift disciples. Those who serve secretly, those who wait, and watch and wonder ...

Luke tells us how, only twenty-four hours earlier, the disciples had been asked to make preparations for the Passover meal. They were to go into the city and look out for a man carrying a pitcher of water, who would lead them to the house where they would celebrate supper that night. I will never forget the first time I entered into this scene in imaginative prayer.

The man with the pitcher had a great deal to tell me. He was a man in grey, a faceless, frightened man, terrified of the consequences of making this quiet, but dangerous commitment to the one who was upsetting all the official apple carts. Courageously he threaded a path through a city rife with threat. He helped me to face my own fearfulness, and I will always be grateful to him – whoever he is!

Gethsemane is a place of shadows, where the worst can be done, but it is also a dark, gestating place that might give new birth. Amid all the activity of the night there is a coming to birth of secret disciples. Fear still overshadows them, a grey presence round the fringes of their hearts. But the darkness triggers a new urgency. Crisis cracks open the seals of their fearfulness, and courage spills out of the cracks.

Jesus has a 'shadow' of his own, along the Via Dolorosa. Simon of Cyrene is on his way to Jerusalem for the Passover feast. Perhaps he is looking forward to the weekend, wrapped in his own thoughts, minding his own business, going his own way. Then suddenly, he is unceremoniously seized, and forced to carry the cross of this stranger – this convicted criminal – up to Golgotha. We can imagine the resentment he might have felt as he laboured along the road to Calvary, carrying a burden that he had no reason to see as his own. I have often joined Simon myself, in prayer, along this journey, apparently so undeserved. I have carried the burdens that I too feel have been unfairly placed on my back. I have gone along, grumbling and grousing, until the moment of truth dawned: for all its discomfort and pain, what journey could possibly have brought me closer to the Lord?

And at the side of the dying Jesus, another night shift disciple emerges. A common criminal, justly sentenced, suddenly wakes up to the True Life, dying alongside him. And the awakening is so overwhelming, that he summons the strength to rebuke the abusers and declare himself for Christ. A moment of insight is all it takes to change a tortured dying into horizons of new hope.

Read about these night shift disciples, in Luke 22:7-13 (preparing for Passover), Luke 23:26-32 (Simon of Cyrene) and Luke 23:39-43 (the 'good thief'). Remember what happened to open *your* eyes to the True Life of Christ. Express your feelings to God in your own way.

And after Jesus has been lifted down from the cross, Joseph of Arimathea arrives on the scene. He has forgotten the status and security of his official position. He has forgotten everything except the urgent desire to serve this man Jesus, at the very last moment. We might pause to feel with him the personal cost of his request to take the body for burial. And Nicodemus with him. The man who had once come to Jesus secretly by night to seek his wisdom (John 3:1–2) – we can imagine him slipping through the side streets under cover of darkness to find the man who so powerfully attracted, yet so painfully embarrassed him. Perhaps he thought that he could live two lives concurrently and keep his inner and outer lives safely separated. He must have covered his tracks and made his excuses, been secretive and anxious. Then he found the one he was looking for and nothing would ever be the same again, because the new birth that Jesus explained to him would end the disconnectedness. Jesus had spelled out for him the cost of integrity that night, and he had remained, thoughtful, in the darkness, until the crisis dawned and his hour had come. He might remind us of any similar tendencies and movements in ourselves.

And so we find two men, making bold to confront a menacing authority, because even in his death, Jesus was more to them than their own lives. We watch them make their way by the straight, direct route, to a quiet garden, fearing no one. A secret night shift, living in shadows and dreams. Faith bubbling underground like a subterranean stream, that breaks forth in power when the spear penetrates Jesus' side. Piercing Joseph's skin of respectability, and Nicodemus' anxious searching. Bursting open the door of the upstairs room of the man in grey and opening the eyes of the penitent thief. At the very point when the danger is at its height, it is these night shift disciples, now grown into courageous 'daylight apostles', who make their allegiance known, declaring themselves for the Lord when all the evidence is against him. When his chosen ones are denying him, betraying him, doubting, sleeping, running, these 'accidental heroes' are stumbling into danger and somehow rising to their feet in the middle of the flames.

And so the journey of these last days, that began around the tomb of Lazarus, apparently ends in the garden tomb of Joseph of Arimathea.

Read about Jesus' burial, in John 19:38-42. Notice your own place in the scene, and your own feelings. In silence and sorrow, place in the tomb all your own broken hopes and dreams, your own worst failures and disappointments. Anoint them with the deepest love you have ever known, the greatest desires that have ever inspired you. Water these dead seeds with your tears, if this is how you feel. Then roll the stone across the grave of your dreams, and stay with the darkness. Spend as long in this 'tomb' prayer as you feel drawn to do.

9. THE ACTIVE INGREDIENT

A tiny gladiola shoot is pushing up through one of the cracks in our neighbour's immaculate driveway. Not just any old weed, but a gladiola. My father used to grow prize gladioli, so this little newcomer to the suburban scene attracts my attention especially. I wonder what colour blossom it is holding, tightly wrapped up in that little green shoot, and what a difference it will make to a very ordinary driveway.

Resurrection is not something most of us find easy either to discover or really to believe in. If asked to meditate on the resurrection events described in the Gospels our reactions may range from an artificially induced mood of exhilaration that we feel we *ought* to be feeling, through to the painful awareness of a drab routine, apparently unchanged by the Good News, that so often we really *are* feeling. Does 'resurrection' mean anything at all to us in our everyday living? Does its promise make any difference?

Jesus compares the Kingdom of God with a measure of yeast. This image reminds me of a time of prayer once that took me, in imagination, into a small room at the back of a little cottage. In the room was a large, white, scrubbed wooden table, and rows of shelves around the walls, all stacked with earthenware jars of flour. Nothing else, just flour. On the table was a large mixing bowl.

'They are waiting for the bread,' Jesus seemed to tell me, referring to the many people living in the cottage. I looked round at all the shelves of flour and felt a wave of despair. 'I'll be here for ever,' I thought, 'turning all this flour into bread. They'll be waiting till they starve.' Then Jesus came over, and my anxiety subsided. 'They only need one loaf at a time,' he reassured me. And one loaf seemed much less of an impossibility.

Then he measured out the flour, scoop by scoop, and he seemed to be scooping my experience out of those jars – my memories, my regrets, my longings and my fears. And as he scooped, my tears began to flow, spilling

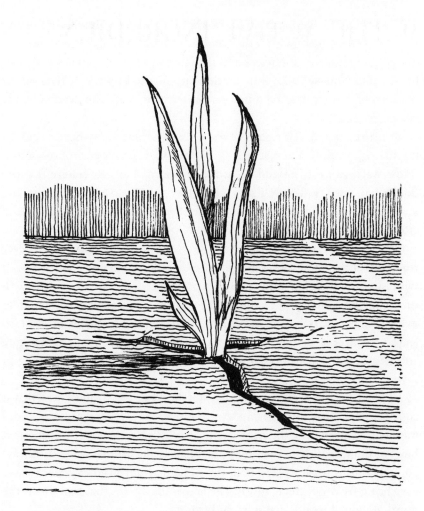

Life will always prevail,
through all the layers of
death in which we try
to contain it

unchecked into the rising mound of flour, making wet, salty patches. 'Now you can knead it,' he said. 'The salt and the water come from the heart of your experience.'

Kneading. The hard, hard work of kneading. And needing. The pressing needs of others. My own pressing needs. I kneaded all the needs into the dough, and gradually the needs and the tears and the salt came together to form a sticky messy ball, a little world that Jesus and I were shaping out of my own life's story. The kneading made my arms ache. The needing made my heart ache.

At last the dough felt right. He took the bowl out of my hands, covered it with a clean cloth and placed it gently in a sheltered corner of the room. 'Now wait with me,' he said. 'Wait for the rising. Do you believe that the dough will rise?' Suddenly I panicked. How could it rise? I didn't put any yeast in it! He gazed straight into my harassed, heartbroken eyes, and came closer – to heal, to console, to encourage.

'You didn't even notice the yeast, did you?' he calmed me. 'You never realised that the yeast was going in, little by little, whenever you have been with me. Simply being in my presence provides the invisible yeast that will turn your kneading into feeding. Like Martha you are worried about so many things, but only one thing is needful. Only a fragment of yeast, to leaven the whole dough of your experience. I am the yeast, penetrating and transforming your dough, silently, invisibly, simply by your staying in my presence.'

We wait for the dough to rise. We watch it and feel it, and know that it is becoming bread for sharing. And always, in every prayer and every moment of awareness, the next batch of yeast is fermenting, for the next bowl of flour. And there will always be more yeast than we will ever need – enough and to spare to leaven all the flour that our lived experience will ever bring us. A gift freely given. The active ingredient that transforms the flour's potential into real and living bread.

When the petals fall

Another memory takes me back to my first retreat. I had spent several days praying the scenes of the Lord's Passion and some painful situations and reactions in my experience had been surfacing into the light of prayer. At the beginning of the retreat a little vase of fresh-cut sweet peas had been waiting to greet me on the desk in my room. These flowers had been such a source of joy and comfort to me through the days of the retreat, their fragrance filling my room. Now I was saddened to see how every day more and more of the delicate petals were falling from the flowers. They seemed to be counting down to the day when I would have to leave this graced time in retreat and return to all the problems I had left behind at home.

When it came to the time, in my prayer, to 'let Jesus die', I found myself up against a huge brick wall. Whatever I did, I seemed to be unable to let my prayer go to the extremes of Calvary, and it was only after a long struggle that I was able, finally, to be present in my prayer to Jesus' final minutes. Afterwards I made my way slowly back to my room. I went over to the window, and realised that the last petals had slipped away from the flowers, and were lying, lifeless, on the windowsill. The tears welled up. The flowers seemed to embody all the sorrow, the anxieties, and the fear of the future that had shaped my day's prayer. But it was then that, through my tears, I reached out to touch the dying flowers, and I felt my fingers running along the beautiful silky seed pod that had been revealed when the petals fell. It was a sign of resurrection. An exquisite silvery gateway to new life. But would it retain its sacramental power when I returned to the challenge of everyday living?

We, too, are reaching the end of our journeying together through the living Gospel. Will this journey make any difference to the living of the journey of our lives? In this chapter we will look at how what we learn from the Gospel writers about the resurrected life of Jesus might connect to our own 'ground floor' experience as pilgrim people, longing for resurrection, yet hardly knowing what we mean by the word.

When I reflect on the events that followed Jesus' crucifixion and burial, I notice certain patterns that give me real hope that resurrection is a here-and-now reality, and not just a remote, supernatural event, or a sequence of sentences in a creed. I see, for example:

- that the resurrected Lord isn't easily recognised, and often comes in the guise of a stranger
- that he retains the signs of his wounding and suffering, and continues to be marked by his experience
- that he comes into situations of despair, disappointment and doubt
- that he comes unobtrusively, never forcing himself upon us, but letting us discover him for ourselves
- that in his presence just a small shift of perspective can make a huge difference to our vision

- that he brings empowerment and commissions us to move on
- that he can't be clung to
- and that, above all, wherever he appears, he makes a difference.

Reflecting on these facts gives me enormous hope.

- In spite of my failures to recognise him, he will still break through my blindness.
- The brokenness in me, that I felt to be such a barrier between us, might be the very place where I find him most readily.
- When I am 'down and out, and running on empty', he is perhaps especially likely to be there with resurrection power.
- I have no need to fear his 'coming in glory' because he will come as gently as a night breeze.
- I don't need to go to the ends of the earth to discover some kind of mystical presence, but instead he is waiting to greet me on my own doorstep, when I am ready to receive him.
- Whatever resurrection asks of me, he himself will empower me.
- It is in the letting go of my limited notions of him that I will be freed to move on to the larger vision.
- And whatever this is about, it is going to make a difference. It is going to weigh me in on the side of Life.

Well, I am rather good at these things – at blindness and brokenness. At being at the end of my rope and bogged down in doubt and disappointment. At limitation and fear and trying to hold on to what I feel safe with. So if these were the very places where the resurrected Lord revealed himself, there is hope for me yet!

Blind encounters

I once walked past my own father in the street, without noticing him, and he, just as embarrassingly, walked past me. It was only a few moments later that we both thought that the person we had just passed looked vaguely familiar, and turned round to see each other for who we really were.

So I have no problem at all in identifying with Jesus' friends who nearly missed him in their post-resurrection encounters with him. The companions on the road to Emmaus, the disciples fishing on the lake near Tiberias, and Mary Magdalene all seem to have suffered from my brand of short-sightedness. What is it, we might ask, that makes us so incapable of seeing things as they are. My own guess is that it is because we tend only to see what we are *expecting* to see – which in my case limits my peripheral vision to about two per cent of reality.

One thing, however, that would break through this impasse would be to feel ourselves personally greeted. If my father had spoken my name as he passed I would immediately have connected to his presence and responded to him. Hearing my name would have broken through the trance-like state in which I so often seem to roam the world. The power of a name is huge. I remember once being present at the celebration of the Eucharist, at a time when I was feeling very depressed and lost. Perhaps I was blindly searching for something of God to cling to, but the service had largely passed me by. I went forward to receive the sacrament, and the person who was offering communion knew me, recognised me, looked into my eyes and spoke the familiar words in a personal and direct way: 'The body of Christ, *Margaret.*' Suddenly it was Jesus standing there, and I had found what I had come searching for. The compassionate greeting of a friend is, truly, the resurrected presence of the Lord.

On another occasion we had been shopping, and become involved in an unpleasant scene in the supermarket car park. When we got home I was feeling shocked and shaken, and I went into the bedroom, for a private cry. After a few minutes my toddler daughter came looking for me. She saw me in tears, and went off again, only to return with her favourite teddy bear, which she placed in my lap. 'Mummy!' she said simply. And the stone rolled away from my tomb, and I could live again.

Small signs, in a big and broken world. But it was just such small signs as these that Jesus himself offered to his grieving friends in the weeks that followed his death. Perhaps bigger signs would be more than we could bear. A blinding flash from heaven might shock us further back into our fearful shells. But the gentle naming of a name, or an unobtrusive invitation to a shared meal coaxes us to the borderlands of new life. This seems to be the way of the Lord, to meet us on familiar ground – where we least expect him!

Read the account of how Mary Magdalene meets the risen Lord in the garden of resurrection (John 20:1-18). Be present to her inability to see who is standing before her, as long as her grief-laden search for all she has lost is dominating her consciousness. Then hear Jesus call her by name and notice how her focus changes. Nothing matters now except to discover anew the lost treasure and open her heart to whatever he will ask of her.

As you reflect on this encounter, allow any memories of your own to surface of times when someone has spoken your name and broken through a veil of sorrow or fear, to bring you new life. These are resurrection moments. Express your feelings to God about them in whatever way you feel drawn to do so.

Broken into wholeness

Right at the beginning of this journey we reflected on the immense beauty that lies concealed inside a simple agate stone, and how each of us is like that. But this hidden beauty is only revealed when the stone is sliced through, and polished. And all too often, the person whose beauty lies within the stone may fail to see its elusive mystery that seems to be concealed beneath layer upon layer of stone. The paradox is that the hidden and particular 'aspect of God' that is held in the core of our being seems only to be revealed when we, too, are broken open by our own personal experience of pain or suffering, physical, mental, emotional or spiritual. We shine with the light of God only when the scouring pads of experience have stripped away our rough edges and encrustations. And when that happens we may be hurting too much to see what is being revealed.

Whenever Jesus appears to his friends after his resurrection, we notice that he is carrying all the marks of his bitter experience – the wounds and scars of the suffering and death through which he has passed. Much as we would wish it were otherwise, there is something about our personal experience of pain that is essential to our growth into the fullness of life. I can remember being told a story once about a young girl of about twelve whose parents thought she had a good singing voice. They were so convinced of this that they consulted a well-known musician and asked him to hear her sing, and give his opinion about her musical potential. The girl sang her best, and afterwards the tension ran high as they awaited the expert verdict. Finally he spoke. 'She sings well,' he said. 'When her heart has been broken, she will sing sublimely.'

Do we want that kind of resurrection? Will it be worth the heartbreak, to sing our true song? Will our deepening understanding of the power of the risen Lord be worth the breaking open of our lives that alone will reveal it? The pearl of great price, it seems, is often buried in a tightly sealed oyster shell. Do we long for the pearl more than we dread the pain of having our oyster broken open? Does our desire outweigh our fear? And when we realise that resurrection beckons us, will our trust in God be stronger than our self-doubt?

Read the account of how Jesus appears to Thomas, the doubter, in John 20:24-9. Jesus addresses Thomas' doubts not by giving him a lesson in theology, but by insisting that he put his hand into Jesus' wounds – that he quite literally *gets in touch with* the pain that is the price of the True Life.

Take some time to get in touch with your own life's woundedness, trusting that it is precisely there that you will find the evidence of resurrection. Go back in your prayer to times in the past when you have felt overwhelmed by your problems and reflect on how, in some way or other, you came through that experience, to arrive at where you are today. As you recall the pain, hear Jesus' words, over and over, spoken directly to you: 'Peace be with you. Move beyond your doubting and self-doubting, and trust me. We have come this far together, and however you are feeling now, I am with you. My woundedness is holding yours, and my resurrection is leading you to Life.' Let these experiences, remembered in the Lord's presence, strengthen your trust that he will continue to nurture you with his own risen life, and that he is holding out a deeper security to you, below the depths of your darkest doubts.

Out of the depths

The people who encountered the risen Lord in the period following his death were far from being in buoyant mood. We, who know the 'end' of the story, may find it impossible to imagine how it might have felt, to have put all your trust in this one man, to have committed your whole life to him, only to see him executed like a common criminal. Those who have never known the terror of being 'wanted for questioning' in a totalitarian regime cannot begin to guess how it might have felt to be implicated in the mission of a man who had been crucified for sedition. And so we find

Jesus' friends going to ground, to nurse their fear, their disappointment, their despair. Most of us have likewise 'gone to ground' at some point, and wanted the earth to swallow us up, in our need to escape from some personal anguish, and nurse our desire just to curl up and die. If this is a state of mind that opens us up to a meeting with the risen Lord, then perhaps we are better qualified than we thought.

Perhaps I can tell you about Nicholas, whose story is painfully true, though I have changed his name. Nicholas had worked for twenty-six years for the same company, and was a respected member of the technical staff. Then he was made redundant. By the time his day of departure arrived, most of his immediate colleagues had gone ahead of him into the streets of uncertainty. Now, as many of you will know, the smell of redundancy is a bit like the smell of death. No one wants to get too close to it. Perhaps we are afraid that it may be contagious. On his last working day, Nicholas was alone in the office. No one came near. Perhaps no one thought about it, and if they did, they wouldn't have known what to say. The hours ticked past, and Nicholas' outer shell was feeling more and more fragile. Then the phone rang. 'How are you doing?' a former colleague asked him – one who had walked the plank a few weeks earlier. The kind words dissolved Nicholas' resolve, and he broke down on the phone.

Half an hour later, Nicholas left the place where he had worked for half his life. He left by the back door. He left unnoticed and unacknowledged. A Calvary experience. He might well have asked, 'Where is God in this?' If this question was in his mind, the next day was going to provide an unexpected answer.

The alarm went off as usual. The habits of a lifetime die hard. Nicholas showered and shaved, and as the truth of his new situation hit him, he felt his legs crumpling up beneath him. It was then that he found himself remembering that since he was eighteen he had never started a working day with nothing to do. The thought turned from 'I am redundant' to 'I am free'. It was a far from joyful turnaround, but it was just a tiny sliver of God getting through a hairline crack in the despondency. He took himself to town to sign on at the Job Centre. After this further experience of humiliation, he happened to bump into one of the homeless people he knew, who populate the town centre. The two greeted each other, and Nicholas invited Terence to come to McDonald's with him for breakfast.

And so the smart, newly redundant executive sat down with the unshaven, inebriated street beggar, over a Big Mac, openly enjoying the discomfiture of the McDonald's manager and the gradual shuffling away of the other customers to a more distant table. 'What are you doing here at this time of the day anyway?' Terence asked him. 'Shouldn't you be at work?' 'No work,' Nicholas replied. 'Just up from the Job Centre. Redundant.'

There was a pregnant pause. 'Good God,' retorted Terence, who couldn't remember the last time he'd slept in a bed. 'You're worse off than

And we recognised him in
the breaking of a
burger bun and the
pouring of a Coke

I am!' Then he put his arm round Nicholas' shoulder: 'I'm so sorry, mate,' he said.

Nicholas remembers that day, and often smiles about it. The day Christ the Consoler met him in McDonald's, in the guise of a street beggar, and let him know that someone was with him in the pain. The day they stopped caring about what the manager thought, and cared for each other instead.

Read the account of how two disillusioned companions met the risen Lord on the road to Emmaus, in Luke 24:13-35. Nicholas and Terence met the Lord in the breaking of a burger bun. Can you remember any moments in your own life when someone broke through to you with hope in the darkness, and a gleam of light at the graveside?

Make your own walk to Emmaus. Let the Lord come alongside you, and tell him about your own heartache. Roll out all your disappointed dreams. Share the story of your life. Now let Jesus sit down with you and show you how all these things have been leading you to this moment, to your personal encounter with his resurrected presence. When you reach the crossroads, what will you do next? Is there anything you want to say to Jesus as he walks alongside you in your prayer?

From port to starboard

Perhaps we expect 'resurrection' to be a big, bright, booming affair that will bowl us over and make the way ahead abundantly clear. Yet the accounts of Jesus' resurrected appearances conspicuously fail to bear out these expectations. The risen Jesus comes to our earthly living as quietly and unobtrusively as the infant Jesus first came to the stable in Bethlehem. The power of resurrection is contained in the ordinary moment, that we so easily miss, if we are not looking with the eyes of love.

John, the beloved disciple, has the eyes of love. Had it not been so, it is perfectly possible that the entire boatload of disillusioned disciples would have sailed past their Lord, quite unaware of his presence. They had gone back to the lake to do a spot of fishing and to take their minds off the terrible events they had witnessed in Jerusalem. The antidote to the nightmare was to creep back to familiar territory, and to go through the everyday chores on autopilot.

The stranger on the shore could have been anybody. Even when he called out to them, they didn't recognise him. To his question 'Have you caught anything, lads?' they told him about their abject failure, after fishing all night, and the tone of their reply can probably be imagined. But the stranger wasn't for giving up. 'Try casting the nets over the other side of the boat,' he suggested. When I read about this incident, I often wonder how I would have reacted to this fount of wisdom on the beach, telling me where the elusive fish were swimming! Nevertheless, they did as they were told, and almost sank the boat, so many fish filled their nets. And while all this was happening, one among them was looking at the stranger with the eyes of love, and recognition dawned: 'It's the Lord!' he told them.

What followed was a 'eucharistic feast' on the lakeside. The overwhelming haul was brought ashore, and Jesus grilled fish for them, and broke bread with them. A simpler celebration of such a momentous encounter can scarcely be imagined. 'Come and have breakfast,' he invited them. 'Come ashore, and into a real and living relationship with me that death has no power to undermine.'

This massive transformation, from despair to overwhelming joy, had come about through a simple shift of perspective. The disciples were not asked to sweep the heavens, or scour the earth in search of their Lord. They were asked merely to move a few feet to the other side of the boat. A slight shift of perspective is sometimes all that is needed to turn our worst sense of failure and loss into a rich harvest of new life and hope. But to make such a shift we have to trust the stranger on the shore and obey the promptings he places in our hearts.

A little story arrived on my computer screen via the Internet the other day, sent on by a former colleague. It described another small shift in perspective that broadcast a huge truth to those who witnessed it. It was about a sporting event for young people. One race was specially for handicapped youngsters, and those with learning difficulties. The signal to start was given, and they all set off. The crowds cheered them on in the normal fashion, urging the leader to keep going for the winning post. Then one of the children fell over. Of one accord, all the others stopped in their tracks, and then turned back, to attend to the fallen friend. It wouldn't have happened in a race for 'normal' children. As it was, the spectators realised that they were witnessing something holy, something beyond the normal, and far surpassing it. They rose to their feet as one, and thundered out their applause for all these damaged children who had given them such an unexpected dramatisation of what it means to be human. A tiny incident. A huge change in the hearts and minds of those present.

In Chapter 5 we looked at the effect of the 'Ninth Decimal Place' – that tiny grain of sand that weighs in on the side of Life, and has the potential to grow into a whole universe of abundant creativity. The story of the disciples' shift from port to starboard is another example of God's 'preferential option for Life' in action, where a few feet of deck mark the difference between settling for death and rising to new life.

Read the account of Jesus' appearance on the shore of Tiberias, in John 21:1-14. Let yourself join the disciples in their sense of futile despair. Go back to your own 'familiar ground' and notice your own strategies for avoiding the worst pain of personal disappointments. Now look across the water to where Jesus is standing. Smell the charcoal fire, and watch the smoke rising. Listen to his voice ringing out across the water. Does he have anything to say to *you*? Is there anything you feel you want to say to *him*?

Bring him any issue in your life right now, that feels like 'fishing all night and catching nothing'. Can you see any way in which a slight change of approach or perception might change things? How might you bring about that change?

Now let Jesus invite you to breakfast. There is more than enough fish, but what are you going to do with it all? What will you do with the excess of grace he is pouring into your heart? It's like the fish; you can't hang on to it. How might you pass it on or share it out, while it is still fresh?

Through closed doors

'When the night has been too lonely, and the way has been too long, and we think that love is only for the lucky or the strong ...'. These words from the song of 'The Rose', made popular by Bette Midler, have a lot to say about our hopes (or our despair) of experiencing 'resurrection'. Even we, who know the 'end of the story', and regularly affirm our faith in it, are often very far from trusting that resurrection is a reality that might turn our own lives upside down – and that every resurrection is not an 'end', but a new beginning.

Which makes it easy, at least, to identify with the group of Jesus' closest friends, huddled together in an 'upper room', numbed by the events of Good Friday, and terrified of the authorities, for whom they themselves might well be the next target. The doors, we hear, were firmly closed, and fear was the driving spirit. For three days Jesus too had been locked into a stranger's grave. We might pause to reflect on the things that lock us in. What fears dominate our own lives, and keep us captive, afraid to live out some aspect of who we really are? What shape do 'the authorities' take for us? Perhaps they are an external force to be contended with, or a relationship in which we dare not express ourselves? Perhaps they are the shadows that haunt our own inner recesses, telling us not to step out of line, warning us to keep our heads down, convincing us that we are not up to very much.

We have to imagine the conversation for ourselves, that was perhaps going on among them. The Gospel writer gives us no clues. We hear only that, in the middle of this crippling fear, Jesus himself was suddenly present. 'Peace be with you,' he said – the Jewish greeting of '*shalom*', that is so much more than a good wish for a quiet evening. *Shalom* expresses the desire that the person receiving the blessing might be *whole* in body, mind and spirit.

The first evidence of this 'wholeness', that Jesus has brought to his friends from out of the grave, is their experience of joy. In spite of the wounds he bears, reminders of a nightmare beyond their worst imaginings, they respond to him with joy – a joy that will prove to be so much stronger than the fear. One moment they are drained of every ounce of life energy, barely daring to exist. The next they are filled with joy, and ready to receive the empowerment of the Holy Spirit that he bestows upon them, with the momentous words of commissioning: 'As the Father sent me, so am I sending you.'

On the shore near Tiberias, this joy was kindled out of the simple obedience to Jesus' suggestion that a shift of perspective might yield great fruits. In the garden, Mary's joy was set free when she heard her name spoken by one who loved her. On the road to Emmaus, hopeless bewilderment was turned to joy when a familiar gesture was recognised in the breaking of bread. In every case, the risen Jesus breaks through the blindness of despair, but always quietly, unobtrusively, patiently waiting to be recognised, gently inviting our response.

I am reminded of an occasion when I was taking communion regularly to a dying friend and his wife. One afternoon we were sitting together round their table. His wife had lit a candle, as she customarily did. As the Eucharistic service proceeded, the candle flame flickered and failed, and eventually went out altogether. We were all aware of the incident, and it seemed to be a tiny dramatisation of the struggle that was going on in that house between life and death. Death, it seemed, would be the inevitable victor. The flame had died. Soon the flame of my friend's life would die too. We knew that, and we all shared in the pain of that moment round the table.

Then the patient stretched out his hand, calmly and slowly, and picked up the spent candle. He turned it upside down and poured out all the molten wax that was choking it. Then he set it upright again, and we watched in amazement as the flame leapt up with new life. No one spoke, but all of us knew what the candle was telling us. In ways we could not understand, life, not death, would have the final word, but only when all that we were clinging to was surrendered and poured away.

Read the account of Jesus' appearance to the disciples in the upper room, in John 20:19-23. Let yourself be there in imagination, and feel with the disciples something of the despair and fear that grip them. Bring your own fears into the scene. Notice who or what is evoking fear in you right now. The source of your fear is on the other side of a locked door. Is there anything you can do to open the doors to your fears? Simply notice how you feel, and what your real desire is in this place.

Now let Jesus come into your locked inner room, with his prayer for your 'wholeness'. How do you feel? Is there anything you want to say to him? He shows you his wounds, and then he says that just as he has been sent by his Father, to kindle a new flame in the darkness of history, so he is now sending *you*. But he doesn't just commission you to go out into the world you fear so much. He gives you the empowerment to do so. He brings a new flame into being, and breathes new life, new hope, into the very heart of your being. Can you remember any times when you have felt, perhaps unexpectedly, that you were able to cross some threshold that you would previously have thought impossible? If so, recall that 'resurrection event' with gratitude, and take hold of everything it means for you.

With empty hands

The Passover has been celebrated, finally and definitively, and, paradoxically, it continues to call for celebration in the personal circumstances of every living 'cell' in the Body of Christ. We have walked a Passover journey in these last two chapters, and now we are called forward into the rest of our lives, not as mourners at the foot of our brokenness, but as carriers of the new life that has poured out of that breaking.

A striking characteristic of Jesus' resurrection appearances is his warning to those who meet him not to try to hold on to him. Thus he tells Mary Magdalene not to cling to him, because he has not yet ascended to the Father. In other incidents he consistently moves people on and refuses to allow them to remain locked in their old fears or false certainties. 'As the Father sent me, so I am sending you', 'Go and feed my sheep', 'Tell my friends that I am going ahead of them to Galilee'.

Perhaps his advice might be summarised as 'Don't cling to what is still earthbound. Move on to all that lies ahead. Trust that this "ending" is indeed a new beginning.'

I once attended a course run by my employer, in a college in a beautiful setting. It was at a time of quite intense spiritual searching in my life, and I would slip away whenever I got half a chance, for a few minutes' peace and solitude in the grounds. One night was especially memorable. It was a frosty February evening, and I was completely alone in the gardens. The jets from nearby Heathrow airport soared noisily overhead, while I was completely still and silent. Just for a moment it felt as though the situation was reversed, and it was I who was flying through space to unguessed-at destinations, and the aircraft that were standing still. Perhaps the power of our soul's flight is like that: so far beyond imagination that even the fastest moving earthbound inventions seem to be motionless in comparison.

When the course ended I felt a sharp reluctance to leave this place where so much had moved on for me in my inner world. I remember walking for one last time through the grounds, during a coffee break, and telling God that I didn't want to let go of this time of heightened awareness. And the response seemed to rise up from somewhere inside: 'Move on, *with empty hands*. Only with empty hands will you be free to receive all the gifts that are waiting for you along the onward pathway.'

Jesus enters upon his own soul-flight some short time after his death and resurrection, in the mysterious event we call the Ascension. Luke describes this moment in his Gospel and again at the beginning of the book of Acts. When I try to enter this scene in my imagination I always feel the acute pain of loss, of bereavement and perhaps bewilderment that I might have felt, had I been there. The beloved friend is being taken out of reach, it seems. Without explanation, he simply disappears into a cloud. Maybe this scene speaks to me because my own 'time with God' so often seems to disappear into the ether when I blow out the prayer candle. My own best intentions to be an agent of Life so often seem to float off and become disembodied.

And, paradoxically, this sense of the soul's journey disappearing fruit-lessly into thin air may be precisely because we have failed to register Jesus' instructions to Mary Magdalene. 'Don't cling to what is still earthbound. It will prevent your moving on into new discoveries of the pathways of Life.' Perhaps I fear 'loss' because I am holding on so hard to what seems so solid, but is actually transient and fleeting. Good health, apparently stable relationships, the continuance of things 'as they are', and even earthly life itself. In reality all these things can disappear with barely a moment's notice. Health can fail alarmingly and rapidly, relationships can break down, political and religious systems can betray us and financial security can crumble, climates can destabilise, and life can end, from one day to another. Small wonder that we are warned not to cling to these fragile holds.

Go back now to the account of Mary Magdalene's meeting with the risen Lord in John 20:1-18. This time focus especially on Jesus' words to her: 'Do not cling to me, because I have not yet ascended to the Father.' Suppose that you were meet-ing the risen Lord in this way, what might he have said to you? Is there anything in your life that he might urge you not to cling to, because it is still earthbound? Be gentle with yourself, and allow the Lord to open your eyes to any earthbound treasure that you dread to lose. Jesus redirects Mary's gaze to the need to share her experience with his other friends. In what ways might he be asking you to move beyond the things you cling to?

Firemaking

An autumn afternoon, and the sun is warm and strong in the garden. A lavender bush still grows vigorously among the fading roses. I take a sprig in my fingers, press it hard and roll it across my skin. It reminds me of other pressures, other kinds of crushing that the year has inflicted. But it also fills my senses with its fragrance. It yields to my pressure, and gives out its scent beneath the friction of my hands. Scent cells loosened, their captive contents set free to pervade the autumn air. Friction brings fragrance. Friction brings fire.

Evening, and a TV documentary shows a Polynesian tribesman teaching a young boy how to make fire. Firemaking is a skill to be mastered on the road to manhood. I watch as he patiently grinds wood against wood. The wood fibres flake and break and turn to powder beneath the relentless friction. It seems a long, long time, but at last there is a faint wisp of smoke. The wood begins to smoulder, ever so slightly. The rubbing and crushing is over now. The wood has yielded up its secret under the pressure. The tribesman's activity changes, from strength to gentleness. He feeds and nurtures the wisp of smoke with bits of kindling, coaxing it like a baby, to accept the unfamiliar food. Nursing it watchfully, guarding its infancy. And his loving care is rewarded by the first lick of a tiny flame. One by one the slender threads of kindling catch light and burn bright and clear.

Incredible, that these tentative little flames, vulnerable to every breeze and in need of constant attention, are at the heart of an island's livelihood, a means of cooking food, firing pottery, forging tools. Incredible that the tiny flame of faith kindled in the darkness of Calvary, and fed with God's promise and our own desiring, should break out in Pentecostal flames that would change the world for ever.

And so we reach that part of our journey when the living wood has been crushed into powder, setting free the secret of its heart of fire. Pentecost. After the long, hard struggle – the Lord's and our own – a tiny flame is kindled, which will provide all the living energy we will ever need, to bring the Kingdom of God to birth on planet Earth.

I will never forget the experience of being in Prague to celebrate the first Easter vigil following the collapse of the totalitarian regimes in Eastern Europe in 1989. For the first time in forty years the people were free to celebrate Easter in the traditional Christian way. We joined them as they gathered outside one of the churches in the city. We watched the

The light that is divided multiplies

Easter fire being painstakingly kindled, and we all lit a taper from it. Then each of us carried our lighted taper into the pitch–dark church. Gradually the church was lit up with a joy that had to be experienced to be believed. The joy of freedom and the promise of a whole new way of being, just opening up out of the darkness of history.

Our personal experience of the coming of the Holy Spirit into our lives may be just as dramatic, or it may be as gentle as a baby's sigh, so silent that we only become aware of it in hindsight, when we start to notice its effects. And 'effects' is what this experience is about. Perhaps the most significant of all the characteristics of 'resurrection' that we have been exploring is the fact that *it always makes a difference*. God's new life, welling up within us will always make a permanent difference to the way we are. It will always move us on a little closer to the person we are becoming, the person we shall, eternally, be. Whether it shows itself as just a tiny new shoot pushing through a gravel path, or a whole new way of living, surging up like a volcano from the heart of a revolution, it makes a difference. Every sign of resurrection, whether personal or universal, weighs in on the side of Life. It assists at the ongoing birth of the Kingdom.

Read about the events of the first Pentecost, in Acts 2:1-20. In your imagination, experience the sound of the rushing wind, and watch the coming of the Pentecostal fire. See how it separates into 'people-sized' flames, like a huge wave of fire dispersing into a million tiny tapers, each of which will carry that fire onwards, along one person's unique and living pathway.

Reflect on the flame of that fire that has been kindled in the taper of your own life. Remember with gratitude the pathway along which you have carried it so far, and entrust to God all that your life's pathway will still reveal, in the light of the flame of his Spirit.

The fire of life that God kindles within you is also the fire of courage, far in excess of the sum total of all your fears. Notice the difference it makes in Peter, timid denier become bold proclaimer. Spend some time reflecting on what specific difference God's presence and power are making in your own life.

The spark of God's Spirit has a particular reason for lighting up each person's life, and it will not return to God, its source, until it has done what it was sent to do. We might do well to take time to reflect on what, specifically, it may be doing in our life? It is streaming through all we do – our work, our play, our relationships, our dreams and visions, our immense potential, that started with a single cell and is growing into a wholeness that only God can imagine. How might we nurture and cherish that spark, in particular ways, like the Polynesian tribesman, allowing it to become a source of warmth, nourishment and vision for ourselves and for the world we live in?

Reflect on the words of Isaiah: 'As the rain and the snow come down from the heavens and do not return without watering the earth, making it yield and giving growth to provide seed for the sower and bread for the eating, so the word that goes from my mouth does not return to me empty, without carrying out my will and succeeding in what it was sent to do.' (Isaiah 55:10-11)

You were born for this!

10. FUNNELS OF LOVE

We began this 'Gospel journey' by reflecting on ourselves as a single cell, full of potential, and, above all, holding a fragment of Godself within us. We might go back now to look at that moment when our 'single cell' was first awakened into life, but to see this unique moment from a different perspective. Imagine, if you can, the whole of creation gathered together, holding its breath, waiting for the Word to be spoken – the Word that is bringing *you* into being.

Perhaps you have been to parties to celebrate the arrival of a new baby, where those who are invited bring all kinds of gifts for the new child. Suppose all creation has been invited to your personal arrival into life. Not just the creation we can see, but the creation that is beyond our sight and our understanding. The invisible realities, the energies of life itself, the movements and inspirations that shape our being. We could call them 'the heavenly host'. All are gathered to celebrate your coming into being. All are waiting to pour their own particular gifting into your life. We might envisage a vast funnel, wide enough at the top to hold everything that all creation has to give you, and at the bottom just a tiny pinprick of life – the single cell that is going to grow into everything you have the potential to become.

This 'funnel of love' is the kind of shape I always see when I read Paul's words in Philippians 2:6-11. It reminds me that this was the pattern of Christ's incarnation, death and resurrection. Which, of course, is also the shape of the journey we have been making. For me it looks something like this:

All creation gathers, visible and invisible, in time and eternity
encircling the Creator, encircled by the Creator,
held in the wholeness of the Mystery
laden with gifts, overflowing with love
yet withholding nothing,
outpouring everything
into just a
single
cell
★

which
grows to fullness
relishing each gift
fulfilling each potential
turning the desire of the giver
into the world of faces, facts and feelings,
spilling new seeds of the Mystery over the earth
giving new and ever-growing expression to the Creator's love,
kindling light out of shadows, life out of no-life, until all shall be Life.

Before we go our separate ways, we reflect in this chapter on all that has come down to us, through the 'funnel', and on ways in which our own lives might become funnels of God's loving for the world around us.

Loving with God's love

When we look at our lives, and our personal gifting, in this light, it becomes obvious that the love that is being poured into us is something alive and active, not just fine words inscribed on ancient manuscript. We could say at least these two things about it:

- It reveals itself *actively*. Its 'word', its promise, becomes embodied in the here and now of creation and of our daily experience. It makes a difference.
- It is a *sharing* of Godself with God's creation. It is the way by which God expresses some unique aspect of God's own nature in created life.

God pours himself into the top of the funnel, and enters the core of our being through the narrow channel that we call our life, our experience. He acts upon us in certain ways, and shares himself in certain ways. He does this for each of us, whether we realise it or not.

If our lives are free enough to let God pass through them, in a flow of grace, then something will pour out of the other end of the funnel. It will show itself in particular ways in which we act, and particular ways in which we share ourselves.

Let's look at some of the ways in which God's love expresses itself in creation:

- God acts as *creator* and shares something of the mystery of his nature in the created world.
- God acts as *evolver* and dream-weaver and calls us to participate in this process of Becoming.
- God acts as *sustainer*, and shares the healing nature of his mystery, caring for creation, continually regenerating what is dying.
- God acts as *personal life-giver*, and shares some unique aspect of Godself with each one of us.

How will we respond?

- We can act *creatively* ourselves, bringing life and love where there is none.
- We can act *co-operatively*, helping to weave God's Dream, letting our lives become fibres in that weaving.
- We can act *healingly*, helping to sustain and repair and nourish God's creation.
- We can act *uniquely*, offering our own personal gifting to the world.

Read Philippians 2:6-11. This is a kind of 'hour-glass' prayer. Notice something of the shape of your own 'becoming' – the gifting that was poured into you and continues to sustain and develop you; the times when your own experience has seemed to pass through a 'zero point', when you felt you couldn't go on any more; and the ways in which your life is giving positive energy and love back into the world around you.

The Welcome Mat: love creating

The first time I gave any thought to the way God's love flows through creation, I happened to be staying in a little holiday cabin that belongs to some friends. In fact now, with hindsight, I have no doubt that it was the experience of staying there that led me to such thoughts in the first place.

The owners of the holiday home had said that we were welcome to use it for a few days, but nothing had prepared us for what we would find there. There were flowers on the table, and a fridge fully stocked with everything we could possibly need to eat. Crates of beer, wine and soft drinks stood on the verandah, where a sunshade and reclining chairs also awaited us. Maps and guidebooks stood ready to help us explore the surrounding countryside, and sturdy walking shoes and waterproofs completed the scene. We could watch their television if we wished, potentially bringing the whole world and its treasures and concerns into our experience. Or we could open the windows and let the immediate world enter our being, in the birdsong, the rustling of the trees, the carpet of summer flowers and the laughter of children playing nearby.

As I sat there on the first evening, it dawned on me that we had come with nothing, yet we had everything. In the best possible way, we were totally dependent on gifts of love for our existence during those few days. We had not earned a penny of the money they had spent to stock up the fridge. We had contributed nothing to the birdsong or the sunlight shining on the distant lake. Absolutely everything we touched or sensed or handled was pure gift. We were floating on a tide of gifting that poured freely and joyfully out of their love. That love was revealed in very solid ways, and it was a sharing of all they had, and everything we might need.

It was a vivid example to me of the way in which we can model our own loving on the sheer creative exuberance of God's love, pouring out into all creation. We can almost imagine God thinking to himself: 'When you have given everything you can think of, then give a little bit more!'

Because what we experienced in our friends' holiday home was a microcosm of what we experience when we arrive in this world as newborn babies. We come with nothing and we receive, potentially, *everything* – though God's 'everything' has to be mediated to us through other human hands and hearts. In ourselves we can do nothing to bring ourselves into life or to sustain that life. Yet we live, and move, and have Being.

If I am tempted to forget this, I sometimes stop to reflect on my evening meal before I eat it. I have done nothing to produce the food on my plate. I haven't tilled the fields, or organised the rain and sunlight. I haven't fired the earthenware plate from which I eat, or forged the cutlery. I didn't generate the power that cooked it, nor did I carve the table on which it is set. Men and women I shall never know have worked in fields I shall never visit to bring me my meal. Sailors and boat-builders, paper-makers and lumberjacks, coal miners and nuclear physicists have worked together in unseen harmony to feed me tonight. Nor does the dependency end in my own generation. People have striven to discover fire, to invent the wheel,

All creation feeds me tonight.
How might I return my
energies for the good of
all creation?

to stand upright. Cells have learned how to reproduce themselves, and connect to each other in myriad networks in myriad brains. Fingers have learned to hold tools, and bones have learned how to form fingers. Stars have flung themselves into space, and their elements have turned into me.

The least I can do, in the face of creation's overwhelming generosity to me, is to add my own pinch of creativity to the vast cauldron of life, and to share my meal, and all that it implies, with my neighbour.

Read Psalm 104, and let yourself imagine God's love streaming down to earth, seeping into every nook and cranny, giving life to every kind of creature. Stay with any of the specific details of this psalm that speak to you especially. Do they bring to mind any of the ways in which God's love is flowing through *your* living? Let yourself feel – and *trust* – the total dependency on God, expressed in verses 27-30. If you feel inspired to do so, write your own soul's song of thanksgiving, or express your response in whatever way feels right for you.

The 'Added Value' Factor: love emerging

Of the nineteen 'Mother's Day' cards I have been given during my daughter's young life one especially still makes me smile. A mother rabbit and baby rabbit are standing in a flower-filled garden. The mother is watering the flowers in the flower-bed. The baby is offering her a lovely bouquet that he has obviously just picked from that same flower-bed. Is he really just giving her back what is hers in the first place? And is that all we can ever hope to do for God – give him back what is his own?

Yes and no, I think. 'Yes', because all we ever have to give has first been given to us. And 'no' because the bunch of flowers the baby rabbit offers is not the same thing as the flowers the mother is tending. The flowers he offers her as a gift are her own flowers, but with Value Added! The added value is the love of the baby for the mother, and the desire to express this love in a tangible way. The bouquet represents something more than the sum of its flowers.

Children are front-line teachers of the art of adding value. Which of us has not at some time been asked for some unlikely assortment of objects: old yoghurt pots, bits of material, scissors, glue and the odd fifty-pence piece to buy what couldn't be begged or borrowed? Predictably, these were going to become a 'present', but what that present was going to look like

*All we can give is what we
have ourselves been
given, but we give it with
the added value of our love*

was wholly *un*predictable. It was part of God's emerging Mystery. Children
will beg for what they want and then create these raw materials into
something no one had ever thought of before. And that is no mean gift to

offer. It is something we can do too, when it comes to responding to God's love and loving each other with that same love.

We might do well to stop and think when we next offer a gift to someone. It seems that we are giving of our own, yet the most elaborate gift we can choose only becomes ours to give because we have used the gifts of intellect, skills and imagination first given to us, either to earn the cost of it or to make it. Those gifts were all there, in potential, in that first single cell from which we emerged, and they came to us down the funnel of love. It is our desire to give and to share what we have with a loved friend that adds the value and perhaps it is the added value that turns mere potential into an emerging, evolving, ever-expanding expression of God's infinite mystery.

When our personal existence on earth is over we will all have made a difference. We are free to choose, moment by moment, whether that difference will be creative or destructive – whether we will contribute to the emergence of Life or to its diminishment. To love with God's love is to leave the world a little fuller of Life than when we arrived. It is to be active participants in God's ongoing process of creation.

Read I Chronicles 29:11-20. Recall some of the gifts you have given to others, and what it was that made it possible for you to give these gifts. What was the 'added value' that you gave of yourself with each gift? Let yourself be the guest of God, and simply spend a little time enjoying God's particular gifts you are aware of right now. Express your response in whatever way feels right for you. Let it be your personal prayer of blessing.

Maintenance in progress: love sustaining; love repairing

All too often, of course, we will make choices that do diminish creation and impede or block the process of God's emerging Life. Then the fabric of creation will need to be sustained, nursed back to wholeness, repaired and regenerated. Biologists tell us that, given time, nature is able to restore and heal itself when it has been exposed to destructive events, even if this means eliminating the species that is causing the damage! Shall the delicate mystery of God's self-emergence be any less resilient? We explored, in Chapter 5, what we might call 'God's preferential option for Life' and the fact that the creative dynamic is continually working to bring better out of poor and best out of better. This is God's sustaining love in action, repairing what we destroy and constantly seeking to share with us his Wholeness.

How might we emulate this aspect of God's loving? Max might help us explore some answers.

Max was a works manager in an industrial plant in Berlin during the Second World War. The company he worked for was using slave labour – young girls taken from their homes in Russia and forced to work for no pay and minimal food in Nazi Germany. Max realised that these girls were hungry. He fixed up an unused office for them and left a little calor gas cooker in the corner so that they could make hot soup for themselves. One of the girls was very weak. She had TB, and Max found another office hidden in the attic, where she could lie and rest, while he covered for her absence on the factory floor. Back at home, he put up a false partition in his own flat, and made a bolt-hole for a Jewish family trying to escape the pogroms. Either of these simple actions would have been sufficient to send Max to the extermination camps himself, had he been caught. In small ways like these Max was weaving something a little bit better out of a situation that was bad. He was doing God's work of sustaining a struggling creation, and he was doing it more effectively than the many people who were merely *talking* about 'the Jewish problem'.

It doesn't have to take a huge act of self-sacrifice to add a spot of God's sustaining loving into the world's heartache. The other day I watched a smartly dressed man, obviously driving to the office. Suddenly he pulled in to the kerbside for no apparent reason. I watched him get out and walk over to the nearby iron palings and retrieve a balloon that had lodged there. He took it carefully back across the busy street and returned it to a crying child who had lost it. Then he got back in the car and drove on, leaving traces of God's compassion all over the pavement!

Read Joel 2:21-7. Hear God's promise to sustain and renew the earth and all its creatures. What have the 'spring rains' and the 'autumn rains' meant for you personally, and how have they nourished your growth? What have the 'locusts' eaten? How do you feel about these losses in your life? Now hear God's promise to restore everything you have experienced as loss and to keep on sustaining you and repairing the damage done to your life and the life of all creation. How can you co-operate with God in this ongoing process?

Love's labours lost?

While in prayer one night in a small chapel I became aware of a little lamp that was standing on the floor near the altar. It was a pottery lamp, with hundreds of small holes pierced through its 'shell'. The light streamed out in lovely patterns, all over the carpet. I had been feeling a bit sorry for myself at the time, thinking of feelings and ideas that seemed to be unable to reach a destination or be returned in mutuality of relationship. The lamp spoke straight into my thoughts. 'Which do you really prefer?' it seemed to ask me. 'That your deepest feelings and your brightest ideas should simply get reflected back to you by someone who recognises and affirms them? Or that your loving should be allowed to spill through all these holes and pour out into the world, even though you may never know where its light-beams land?' I settled for the second option that night, and I haven't changed my mind.

If we are really to become funnels of God's loving, we have to be prepared to let that loving flow through us, and not seek to trap it and receive its echo back continually into our own little space. Perhaps this touches on something of what it means to seek to live for the greater glory of God, rather than in our own reflected glory. Cecilia might lead us further into this secret . . .

Cecilia is bedridden and barely able to breathe without her oxygen cylinders. But she crochets intricately patterned squares in white wool and sews them together to make baby blankets. Good therapy, you might think. But she has a deeper reason. Many years ago, Cecilia lost two babies, who died soon after birth. She still grieves for them. One day she heard that the local maternity unit has to dispose of the bodies of pre-term stillborn or aborted babies in cardboard boxes. So now Cecilia spends her days making beautiful blankets to send to the hospital so that these dead babies can be wrapped in human love before they are sent home to their creator. An ongoing act of pure, silent, unrewarded loving that, for me, perfectly expresses God's constant desire to bring wholeness out of brokenness.

Energy, we learn from the physicists, cannot be either created or destroyed. And the same law surely applies to God's loving, expressed in our love for each other. We may never know where its energising stream is flowing to, but our labours at loving will never be lost. Just as Jesus was taken into 'heaven' at the Ascension seeming to disappear into nowhere, but in reality his loving, creating energy was returning to 'everywhere', constantly seeking a place in which to become incarnate. Every time we choose the 'more loving thing' to do, we make a little of that Christic energy incarnate in our own living.

Read Isaiah 65:17-25. God is creating a new heaven and a new earth, and everything that offers its energy to that end will not labour in vain (v. 23). Reflect on any parts of your life that seem to be 'going nowhere' and gently place them in the circle of light from the 'leaky lamp'. How do you feel about letting your love flow out to unknown destinations? Take a walk, in your imagination, on God's 'holy mountain' (v. 25). Discover your own images of this 'new creation', which is fed and watered by that outflowing love that can never be lost.

When the funnel gets blocked

In our hearts we all desire to be funnels of God's loving in the world. In a sense this is the entire destination of our journeying and it takes us back to that fundamental question that shaped our commitment to the 'Kingdom venture': What do I really desire more deeply? The 'more' of God's Kingdom, or the 'less' of my own? What is drawing me further into God's True Life, and what is pulling me in the opposite direction? What do I need to be freed from, what attachments are blocking my 'funnel'?

'Attachments' – those limpets that cling to the inside of our life's funnel and impede the flow of God's love to the world beyond us – can take many forms, and each of us must discover for ourselves what, precisely, might be clogging up the channel of our living. Sometimes the desire for popularity, or the need for material security, for example, might take over our whole energy, colouring every choice we make, so that we lose touch with the deeper Dream that is drawing us forward. We begin, like Martha, to fret and worry about these lesser things, dissipating our energy and losing touch with the Kingdom Vision that we have chosen, in our deeper being. When this happens we become like trees that divert all their energy into maintaining one or two attractive leaves or branches, and in doing so starve their taproot of its sustaining life energy. So, too, the excessive attention we give to our lesser needs or anxieties can starve the taproot of our being.

The actual nature and name of these many 'lesser leaves and branches' is something we can only discover individually. (This question is explored more fully in the companion book *Landmarks*.) However, there is one big block in the funnel that we are probably all prone to, and this is our human tendency to see the years of our own life as a *container*, rather than as a *channel*. It is natural, and all too easy, to put start and end brackets round our personal life story and regard it as a complete entity in itself. This effectively builds a little dam around our own 'three score years and ten'. It disconnects us from the flow of Life of which our own living is just one little stretch. The temptation then is to build everything up around this little dam, to fence it off, to accumulate good things and fine achievements in it and defend it from the world around it. Or we may spend our waking moments worrying about whether our 'dam' is good enough or pure enough, and have no energy left to contribute our personal 'added value' to the flow of creation.

The 'rich young man' in the Gospel story had this problem (Mark 10:17–22). When Jesus invited him to let go of his own little puddle and become, instead, a part of the flow of the great River of life, he went away sad, because he loved his little puddle so much.

The loving spoonful

Of course we can't deal with big things like 'the river of life'! If we try, we will soon feel tempted to flee back to the safety of our own little puddle. Perhaps the challenge is to 'think big in the small place'. One antidote to the tendency to limit our view of things to our own span of years and our own local boundaries might be to reflect on each day's journeying as a part of a larger flow, into which we can add our own spoonful of 'added value'. Two illusions can work against this:

- We can convince ourselves that the 'whole' is far too big for us to have anything to do with it, and busy ourselves instead with lining our own little part of it with comfort and security.
- Or we can convince ourselves that God will not be satisfied with us until we have, single-handedly, transformed the whole of creation on God's behalf, and then waste our energy in beating ourselves up when, inevitably, we consistently fail in this high endeavour.

Both these extremes put the blocks on what we really *can* do. Which is to add just one spoonful of love to each day's experience as it flows through us – to add one dash of added flavour to the world as our day flows through it. This is much more manageable, and we can reflect, day by day, on that challenge, and how we responded to it. Gradually we become more and more conscious of how we really *can* put something of God's love into action. One loving spoonful can go further than we think, in neutralising the poisons in the river, and nourishing the fish. Like that little blue bag of salt we used to get in our packets of potato crisps, in its own small way it can make all the difference.

A spoonful of love is added to life every time we stop to ask: 'What is the more loving way of reacting to this situation?' If we can act on what we find, in answer to that question, the river will be permanently enriched by our response.

Read the story of the 'widow's mite' in Mark 12:41-4. Your loving spoonful is like that meagre offering that meant so much, and that Jesus valued so highly that he pointed it out as an example of someone who was loving with God's love. What does your 'mite' consist of?

Read the parable of the salt in Matthew 5:13. Look back over the last few days. Can you see any moments when you were able to add a pinch of love to the world's crisp packet? Has the salt of your loving helped to melt one of the frozen roadways of the wintering world? Can you see any opportunities you missed? Don't judge yourself, just notice, and reflect.

Now read 'what Yahweh asks of you' in Micah 6:8. 'To act justly, to love tenderly, to walk humbly with your God.' This has been the entire pattern of our Gospel journey, and it can become the pattern for our lives. God doesn't ask us for the earth. He *gives* us the earth, and asks only that we enrich it by one gram of loving.

Surrendering the 'less' for the sake of the 'more'

Nevertheless, letting go of what we think is so essential to our well-being can be very hard indeed, and surely no one ever completely manages it. A prayer familiar to many Christians begins, 'Take, Lord, and receive . . .' and it then goes on to surrender some of the things that commonly tend to block our funnels, so that love can flow freely through our lives and out into the world again. It is a radical prayer, not to be offered lightly. In it we express the desire:

- to give back to God all that is 'less' (which will usually feel very important to us in the immediate space of everyday living) and
- to become open to receive his infinite 'more', even though this may feel very remote and insubstantial from the perspective of our everyday world.

The prayer suggests these things, which are clearly good in themselves, as potential funnel-blockers:

- our liberty,
- our memory,
- our understanding,
- our will,
- everything we think we 'own'.

At first sight the prospect of surrendering these things is clearly preposterous. And even if it were reasonable to surrender these things, in ourselves we would be quite unable to do so. We might, however, express, in whatever way we can, at least the *desire* to surrender them, if they are really blocking our growth, and to offer ourselves and all we are to the call to give birth to God in our world. But before we do so, let us take a closer look at what such a surrender is really asking of us.

Take, and receive my liberty . . .

My liberty is very precious to me indeed. It is precious to us all. So precious that oceans of blood have been spilled in its defence. But what were we really defending? Our liberty to do things our way? Our liberty to impose our way on others? Our liberty to live as islands, regardless of the needs of the bedrock wholeness of creation? The freedom of the children of God is something very different, and only one person's blood needed to be spilled in its defence.

Take, Lord, all our false notions of liberty, our limited ideas of what it means to live free, and give us your freedom, to live for the whole, and not for our own little part.

Take, and receive my memory …

Even more alarming! How, we might ask, can we possibly function without our memory? Surely God doesn't want to reduce us all to zombies. In fact the loss of memory, and the onset of dementia, is probably something most of us dread above all!

Suppose, however, that God were inviting us to be free of the bad programming that memory can hard-wire into our minds? When I look back to childhood I realise that I learned particular coping mechanisms for dealing with the situations in which I found myself. Now, as an adult, whenever anything at all problematic crops up, my mind automatically invokes these programs. It replays the same old tapes. And so I find myself making today's choices using yesterday's data.

Common examples of 'old tapes' are what I call:

• The Three Cs: *conceal, contain, collude.*
• Or the Three Ds: *deny, divert, disown.*

So, for example, I may find myself acting secretively, or trying to prevent some awkward fact escaping into the wider world, perhaps in the service of some false loyalty, but in situations where these coping mechanisms are completely inappropriate. In doing so I am becoming a colluder in a course of action that prevents a problem from being openly addressed.

Or I may catch myself denying that a particular problem exists at all. And if I begin to doubt my own denials, the next step may be to disguise the facts to fit my false view of things, or to project the problem on to someone else, so as to avoid responsibility for it. I dismiss the matter as being 'not my problem', and whatever small redemption its resolution might have brought about is aborted.

Take, Lord, my database of old tapes, so that I might be free, in every new choice, to choose the more loving way appropriate to the situation, freed from the power of my old hard-wired memories.

Take, and receive my understanding …

Well, dementia has thoroughly set in by now. Is that what we want? Of course not! But what if God were inviting us to stand back from our own limited understanding of things, and become open to his deeper, all-reaching Understanding.

We can touch into what this might mean if we reflect on the ability of our teenage children to put us right on every aspect of how the world functions. We know what they have yet to discover – that their understanding is pathetically incomplete. And we are only a few years further on than they are! The joke sums it up: 'Hire a teenager, while he still knows everything!' The destructive forces within and around us might say the same thing: 'Get hold of her now while she still thinks she knows it all. This is when she'll do the most damage!' God knows better. He is prepared to wait!

Take, Lord, my certainties, and give me the grace to be open to your Mystery. The more I know I don't know, the more I have to learn from you.

Take, Lord, my entire will ...

So does God want to turn us all into doormats? I don't think so. Was Jesus a doormat? When I listen to the News I begin to understand what it means when everyone is working out their own will. Take any political hotspot and it isn't difficult to see how one side's 'will' is the other side's oppression. Human 'will' almost always revolves around the personal 'kingdom' of the person making the decision.

We are all caught up in these self-focused structures and institutions – even in the church! So to surrender the 'will' of these lesser kingdoms to the Dream of God's Kingdom is one of the most radical things we could be asked to do. We can only do it in the power of the Holy Spirit, and with the help of constant and honest discernment.

Take, Lord, my determination to make things fit the needs of my personal kingdom, and refocus my gaze, moment by moment, on the Dream of your Kingdom.

Take, Lord, and receive, everything I regard as 'mine'

What a grasping God we serve? Not at all! As we have seen, at some length, in this chapter, everything we call 'ours' is pure gift. Go to the old family photo albums and take a look at what you brought with you when you were born! A joke phrase that we might do well to take more seriously runs, 'Close your eyes, and everything you see is yours.'

The hidden secret of this statement of surrender is that what we think we own is so very much less than the infinite potential in which we share when we receive every gift as God's outpouring of life and love for the common good of all creation. The real riches consist in letting it flow through our life's funnel, adding our own value to it as it passes through.

A rather inadequate analogy might be to think of the difference between trying to communicate with one other person over a distance using smoke signals, and surfing the Internet where, potentially, we have access to all the world's information, not merely that one person's stumbling messages. And where we can add our own wisdom to the web, for the benefit of all. Letting go of a jealous sense of ownership of what we think is ours doesn't *diminish* our treasure. It *expands* it by a multiplication factor equal to every gift God has ever given, or ever will give, to any of his creatures. It turns our perceptions inside out, to reveal a golden lining.

Even the profit-driven stock market knows this much: to own one share is nothing, but to have a part in the enterprise of an entire company is infinitely more valuable, more dynamic, more open to growth. Nothing less is offered to us: when we surrender exclusive ownership of our own little 'share' of resources, both material and spiritual, we become co-creators in the Kingdom of God.

Take, Lord, everything I have and call my own. Take every gift, and use it in the service of your Dream. Give me the grace to surrender all that is partial and fleeting, and become free to receive your wholeness and completeness.

Write (or draw!) your own version of (or response to) the 'Take and Receive' prayer.

Take, Lord, and receive,
All my liberty,
My memory,
My understanding,
My entire will,
Everything I have and call my own.
You gave me every gift,
And to you I return them.
Use each one entirely according to your will.
Give me only your love, and your grace,
And that is enough for me.

The gliders and the helicopter

At the end of Chapter 9, as we moved into the final stage of our walk with
Jesus through the events of his earthly life, we watched him disappear into
thin air. It was an experience, perhaps, that often recurs in our daily living.
Closeness to God, sometimes almost palpable, can seem to vanish as
quickly as it came. We can't hold on to the feelings, and sometimes it seems
that all we have left is the knowledge that once we *knew* God's presence
and God's action in our lives, and such knowledge can never be denied.

When I start to wonder which is the more real, the river of God's love
streaming through creation, or the problems and anxieties of my personal
puddle, I remember an incident that happened one afternoon while I was
enjoying a late summer stroll.

I began my walk by climbing a path up a gentle hillside. I was deep in
thought, and barely conscious of the breeze caressing my skin and the blue
sky stretching out above me. Perhaps my thoughts were focused a little too
much on the path I was walking, rather than on the world that path was
passing through.

However, something stopped me in my tracks. I became aware of three
gliders hovering overhead. Their calm presence and graceful movements
fascinated me. They rose and sank with the thermal currents. They let
themselves be carried on the invisible energies that were holding and
guiding them. They were utterly unobtrusive, yet they penetrated deeply
into my awareness.

Something within me wanted to be with them, a part of their balanced,
measured, joyful motion. I realised how much I wanted to allow myself to
be carried on God's currents, and trust him for the cosmic dance that
would unfold, in which my life would have some part. I wanted to carry
their kind of silence in my heart – not the silence of isolation, but the
silence of relational and all-inclusive loving that doesn't need to say
anything about itself, but simply needs to be.

I walked on a bit further and came to a field, where a huge and
powerful shire horse was kept. I knew him, from other walks along this
path. I thought we were friends. He was a gentle giant – everyone knew
that. My eyes went back to the path again, and my mind returned to its
preoccupations. The next thing I knew was that the good-natured horse
was bolting like a thing demented, diagonally across the field, heading
straight for where I was walking. In his blind panic he was obviously quite

unaware of my presence. I leapt into the hedge to escape his thundering hooves. He galloped past, missing me by inches. Then he came to rest in a little coppice, quivering, his eyes wild with fear, gazing in terror up to the sky.

My eyes followed his gaze, and I saw a helicopter overhead. This was clearly the root cause of his panic attack. And I could see why. The experience of the helicopter was about as far removed from that of the gliders as it is possible to imagine. The gliders had been present to me in such a gentle, non-invasive way, speaking their meanings in silent eloquence. The helicopter came buzzing through the skies like an angry hornet, driving an aggressive trail of noise through the quiet of the afternoon, taking over everyone's consciousness and, for a few short minutes, seizing everyone's attention, infecting everything around it with its frenzy.

Unlike the shire horse, I knew about helicopters, and how they would go away again eventually, leaving the countryside in its more permanently peaceful state. But for the horse the helicopter seemed to be the whole of reality for those few terrifying minutes. He reacted to the intrusive presence as if it were a mortal enemy with the power to take him over and destroy him. In his fight for survival, the horse would have been capable of destroying anything that got in his way, as I almost found out to my cost. And once he had reached the illusory 'safety' of the little coppice, he stood trembling like a frightened foal – a fine and powerful creature reduced to a jelly by something that for me was just a passing irritation.

It was becoming all too obvious to me, as I watched this scene unfolding, that I can react like that too, when passing tidal waves stir the calm of my personal puddle. What seems to me like a terrifying threat, in the small place of my own little world, is actually just a momentary disturbance, in the context of the greater reality. Perhaps it's all a question of perspective.

What our life's 'Kingdom journey' offers us is something of the perspective of God. It frees us to move with the currents of God flowing through our lives, rising with our inspirations, sinking with our experiences of emptiness, but never falling out of the great cosmic dance. If we can part with the excess baggage that weighs us down, this perspective can raise us to a level of awareness that can see the intrusive hornets of our fears and compulsions for the passing disturbances they really are. It reminds us, day by day, that the bedrock truth of God's presence is the permanent state of our being.

Our 'helicopter' experiences will always have the power to fly through our consciousness, and temporarily destabilise our journeying. But they can also help us to grow, as we learn to discern their root causes and correct our course accordingly, and they are never the final word. The 'gliders' will still be there long after the noise of the 'helicopter' has passed.

Snail's pace to eternity

I visited the Gallery of Old Masters in the city of Dresden not long ago. There I came across a fifteenth-century painting of the Annunciation by Francesco del Cossa. Among the very many representations of the Annunciation hanging in the gallery, this one caught my attention in a special way. It wasn't the stylised figures of Mary or of the angel that struck me. Nor was it the intricate detail of the architecture or the careful blending of colour and light. No! What caught my gaze, and made me smile, was the image of a little snail crawling along the floor as Heaven announced its Coming to Mary of Nazareth.

Who knows what the artist intended by including this tiny creature in his altarpiece? But I have often reflected since then on what that snail has to say to me, and why it attracts me so much.

For one thing, it reminds me that I am crawling across the landscape of eternity in my own little pilgrimage of life. Heaven and earth may be coming together above my head, to change the entire destiny of humankind, but all I can see is a small corner of the pattern of just one of the tiles on the floor. Next year I may get to see a fragment of another corner. No way will I ever take in the awesome mystery in which the Artist has so unaccountably included me.

And so I plod on. My horns are stretched out in front of me, trusting that I will pick up whatever signals I need for the next inch of the journey, and praying to discern their meanings for my life. Everything I think is 'mine' – including my rather skewed understanding, my mightily obstinate will and my miniscule notions of 'God' and 'God's ways', are all packed up in my 'mobile home'. I have to contain things, you see, because I am human, and that's what humans do – but I have at least got as far as understanding that my 'container' must be portable. Like the ark of the covenant,

Unaccountably included in the picture, by the creator of the snails and the stars

it is my way of getting a handle on 'God'. I carry it with me through the slow progress of my journey, retreating into it from time to time to refresh my inside knowledge of times when God has been so very present to my experience.

... Time for all of us to move on, knowing that what our hearts are exploring is a canvas infinitely greater than our imagination can contain, but leaving, perhaps, a little silver trail behind us, where some of God's love spilled out and touched the world and made it shine a bit – a signal that this small stretch of time and space we call our life is also being walked by Christ.